PERCEPTION
Experiencing the Wonders of Life

Namrata Pandya

ISBN: 978-1-5272-2887-0

First published 2018

Copyright © 2018 Namrata Pandya

CONTENTS

PERCEPTION

Experiencing the Wonders of Life

Inspired by and Dedicated to Khushil

Life can be beyond imagination, and is often unpredictable. However, one thing is for sure – it is full of surprises. Whether these surprises are wonderful or shocking, we must learn to roll with the punches, and embrace the greatest moments.

My son, Khushil, had a saying for life's surprises – 'So what?' Khushil did not let life's surprises phase him. He did not let them knock him back, and in doing so he proved an inspiration to us all.

This book is dedicated to him.

INTRODUCTION

What if I told you that I am 14-years, 8-months, and 27-days-old, and suffering from a terminal brain tumour? The tumour has affected my eyesight, and caused loss of speech. I cannot swallow, I have zero mobility, and my hands don't work. If I want to move or hold my head up, my parents have to carry me. I have been suffering from this tumour since the 26th March 2015 – and my condition has gradually deteriorated. If I told you all of this, what would you say?

If you are thinking, 'Poor you' then let me say this – you are wrong. My tumour may have taken my physical abilities away, but it can never take my determination, or my power to live life with full spirit. I look at my life, and my diagnosis, and I see the positives. I see an opportunity. I am the only person who has an idea of when my end is going to be. How many other people have this opportunity, this chance, to do everything they'd like to in their life?

I look around and see that I have so many good people around me. I am not going to let my tumour dictate my life. I am going to live my life, on my terms.

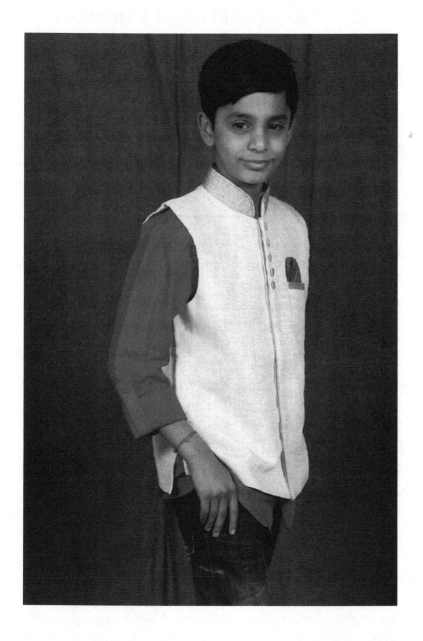

Dad's Diary for his Best Friend – his son Khushil
(Bhavesh Pandya)

"Take a breath, close your eyes wherever you are. Desist mediocrity and then promise yourself that you will move forward. Ad infinitum…"

Khushil was my world. He was my pride and joy, and life without him is not the same. However, since he died, I have never felt that he is not with me.

When Namrata decided that she was going to write this book, I have to be honest and say that I hoped she wouldn't. I was not ready to live the two years and six months again without Khushil. On top of that, Namrata is very sensitive. Writing this book meant that she would be upset and cry a lot – something which Khushil and I never wanted to see. Ultimately, however, I supported her. Deep down, I know that this is the right thing to do, and that it will prove a fitting legacy for my best friend – my son.

I don't know where to start writing about Khushil. Khushil was a dream child, and both Namrata and I know that we were lucky to be called Khushil's parents.

No one can ever take his place in my life. We used to share all our secrets with each other. But there was one thing that he never shared, and that was how he felt about his brain tumour. Khushil was a very caring and sensitive boy. He would always make sure that Namrata and I felt looked after, and would never say anything that would worry us. He knew that if he was to share

8

his feelings, it would hurt us. So, like a mature person, he kept them in his heart and never let them out. This was a very brave thing for a 14-year-old to do, and I am extremely proud of him.

Khushil never called me Dad, he always called me Bhavesh. I did used to tease him on this, but he would say, 'What does that mean? I will never call you Dad, you are my Bhavesh and I will not call you Dad even in my dreams!' I am lucky that I was able to be my son's best friend, and I will forever be grateful for this.

Just like friends, we used to fight and argue a lot over little things, like which channel to watch on television, which restaurant to visit for dinner, which ice-cream to buy, and so on. Khushil's main aim was to annoy me, and it was the same from my side! We used to hide each other's things, like clothes or watches, and we'd spend at least an hour in bed during weekends once we woke up. It was our personal time. We used to call it "Guchi Guchi" time.

Khushil with Bhavesh, 2006

Let me tell you about a very funny incident. Khushil would never let me select his birthday gifts. He would always let Namrata get whatever she liked, but I wasn't allowed to choose. On one occasion I kept telling him, 'I've got you a surprise for your birthday', and then giving him hints about how he would use my present daily, and there wouldn't be a day when he wouldn't need it. When his birthday arrived, I gave it to him – a fresh pack of toilet rolls. You should have seen his face. He didn't talk to me for over half-an-hour, and then I gave him his real gift – a PlayStation 4. Khushil was extremely happy, but he refused to believe that it was my choice, saying that Namrata must have picked it!

One thing I loved about Khushil was that he was never greedy. In fact, he would never ask at all – it was Namrata and I who bought him things. I can never remember Khushil buying more than one game at the store. He would say, 'One is more than enough.' Thinking back on this, I believe that my son showed an incredible level of maturity for one so young. He just had a very different view of life. He was never overly attached to any one person, but at the same time never let himself become too happy or sad. He always stayed neutral. I remember one occasion when we had just returned home from India. I asked Khushil, 'Do you not feel sad when we come back from India? Everyone in India loved you.' In response, Khushil said, 'For me, you and Mum are the most important. Nothing else bothers me. I am happy if someone is with me, or someone visits us, but at the same time I am okay when they leave.' When he said this, I instantly knew that my son was exonerated. He was not tied down to anything, nor was he overly reliant on anyone else. He was his own person, and for that I am still immensely proud.

Khushil and I were very competitive with each other, and whenever we played games we would play to win. Namrata always supported Khushil, of course. We used to play all sorts of games – badminton, table-tennis, football, plus games on the PlayStation and Xbox. Khushil always made a point to try and do everything that I was doing, and beat me at it. If I was painting the doors of our house, he would want to do the same. I was using a bigger brush to paint, he would want the same. If I was washing the car, he would want to wash as well. When he was little he was not able to reach the top of the car, so he would make me pick him up while he did it. When he was diagnosed with a brain tumour, I used to let him win sometimes, but he didn't like that. He would say, 'Leave it, Bhavesh, I don't want to play. You are not playing properly.'

While we used to play a lot, we also studied together, as per Khushil's schedule. Khushil was brilliant at Maths, and it was always a pleasure to teach him. When I used to tell him that I got 93/100 Marks in Maths (GCSC), he used to say, 'I am sure you cheated. You would never get these marks on your own.'

We had a habit that I would get Khushil into bed, and that was part of our bonding time. It would normally take me forty-five minutes to get him to sleep when he was younger. Bed time was when we would tell each other how our day had been. Khushil would start his day from when I dropped him off at school, until the last lesson. I would then tell him how my day had been. This was always our routine. There was never a change in this, no matter what time he went to sleep.

As Khushil grew up, sometimes he would make me go to sleep before him, and then call Namrata and tell her, 'Look Mum, he doesn't want to talk to you. He does not like you anymore. I would never do that to you. I am telling you I would not tolerate this; you have to take some action against this type of behaviour. You are very soft and very nice. He's taking you for granted!' He loved trying to get me in trouble with Namrata, in fact it was one of his favourite things to do! We used to talk about my school days, but only up until year 10. Khushil, naturally, would always want to know about year 11 and my college life. I used to say to him, 'I will tell you once you are in year 11', and then after his diagnosis we finally got around to talking about it. He then asked me, 'Does Mum know what you were up to?', to which I replied, 'Not to the extent that you do.' From that day on, he used to tease me, saying, 'If you annoy me then I will tell Mum everything about your year 11!', but he never did.

Namrata and Khushil had a very special relationship. Khushil never had to tell her if he needed anything – she would just know. She understood Khushil so well that if Khushil wanted to tell her something, but couldn't, she would go to him and say, 'I know there's something you're not telling me.' Another caring thing that Namrata did, was that she'd always taste medicine first, before giving it to Khushil. She wanted to make sure it was safe, and to check whether Khushil would enjoy the taste.

Even though Khushil and I were very competitive, Namrata used to get involved too! She would watch cartoons with him, play games, and behave as if she knew nothing, and then Khushil would teach her how to play. She would also fight for ice-cream and teddy bears with him, and sometimes they would be so childish that they'd fight for the same place on the sofa. They'd even fight for my affection! Sometimes they'd ask me, 'Bhavesh, who do you love more?' and then I had the dilemma of choosing.

In short, Namrata and Khushil had a very unique bond – one of love, care, competition and emotional need for each other. I know that Namrata loved Khushil more than words can say, and part of my pain comes not just from my loss, but hers too.

As a parent, Khushil and Namrata used to tell me that I am a very good stage actor. I'd have to agree with that. Many times I sat in front of Khushil at the table, feeling overwhelmed by everything that was happening, but I managed to control myself and give him a smile. However, if I am a good stage actor, then Khushil is a master. As you will see from this book, Khushil's strength, composure and all-encompassing care for us, his parents, even in the face of such adversity, was absolutely remarkable. Khushil had the courtesy and modesty to make Namrata and I feel completely in control, even though he was making the big decisions, and in doing so showed incredible maturity.

Namrata and I learnt so much from Khushil. He taught us how to love life, and how to keep fighting, never losing spirit in any situation. He taught us how to accept the trials that life throws our way, and live with a smile on our faces. He also taught us that, when finding yourself in a situation that you can't do anything about, it is best to find a way to live through it – without mourning. Khushil had an incredible ability to read faces. He used to be able to tell, just by looking at us, whether we were unhappy or worrying too much. On those occasions, he would say, 'Don't worry too much, be my normal Bhavesh.' In this way, Khushil gave us the strength to get through what was the most difficult period of our lives, and his words still help us today.

Normally, even when times were hard, the three of us would get through the day just laughing and having fun. But on the 6th August, when we were taking a selfie, all three of us ended up in tears. Namrata and I felt helpless. We were seeing our one and only son deteriorate, and were unable to do anything about it. I asked Khushil, 'Is there anything that you would like me to do?' And then I apologised to him, because I wanted so much to do everything I could to make him better. In response, Khushil said, 'I don't want anything from either of you. You have both done everything you can. You are the best parents in the world.'

When Khushil was first diagnosed with a brain tumour, and we were told the symptoms, we were always worrying about how he would adjust to crutches, or having a wheelchair. But Khushil showed us that it really is possible to accept something this hard, and move on. He did not let the physical disability dictate his life. He didn't let himself stop, or mourn, he carried on as he always had – enjoying life to the full. To this day it still amazes me that a 14-year-old boy could be so flexible. From adapting to using a wheelchair, to using an NG tube for feeding, there was no end to the disruption – but Khushil just took it all in his stride.

Now, when I feel down, I don't need to read an inspirational quote or a book to make me feel better – I just remember Khushil, and that alone gives me strength.

Khushil often used to say to me, 'You are not strong enough.' He was correct in that. I would never talk about his tumour, not even with Namrata. I used to feel scared about the end result, and was afraid of how we'd cope with it. In contrast, my wife is a remarkably strong person. I can't imagine any mum being as strong as she has, living life in the way she did, knowing that her only son would not live for much longer. More than I have, Namrata has been able to take Khushil's words of wisdom and run with them. She lives life with a smile on her face. She didn't just look after Khushil, but after me too. I cannot thank God enough for giving me such a wonderful family.

As Khushil used to say, 'Buy one, get two free. It's either all three of us, or none of us.'

When someone asks me about what life is like without Khushil, I struggle to answer the question. As I said, I have never felt that he is not with me, but at the same time I do miss ironing his clothes, playing with him, having friendly fights, applying hair oil, and many more things that I can't do now. I have always believed that if anything bad happened, then it could be a good thing for future, as we can never understand what God has planned for us. I lived my whole life believing this. However, on this occasion I must confess that it is hard to see the light, after God took my one and only son from me – in a way where I could do nothing, and felt helpless. But I know that Khushil would not want me to think like this, and so every day I am striving to follow in his footsteps, and not lose hope.

The quote at the start of this chapter was the final message I received from Khushil, before he passed away. Just as Khushil wished, I have promised myself that I will move forward, and help Namrata to do the same.

Khushil and Bhavesh at home, December 2014

About Namrata

I am Namrata Pandya, writer of this book, and Khushil's mum. In terms of identity, I prefer to be known as 'Khushil's mum' and would quite gladly take this title for the rest of my life. I am a wealth management advisor, working for HSBC Bank. I have been advising clients for over 10 years now – not only helping them to plan their finances, but also helping them to protect their family and livelihood. In the past, I have also worked as a teacher, cashier, personal banking advisor, savings specialist, and also as a self-employed businesswoman in India.

My son, Khushil, was an extraordinary individual. I'm not only writing this book to extend his legacy, but to show others how to smile, stay positive, and believe in overcoming adversity. Khushil was an incredible example of all of these things, and I believe that he set an example for others in the way he lived. Khushil showed us how simple it is to smile.

I sincerely hope that this book inspires you to live life to the full, and enjoy each and every second of your time on this earth.

Now, I'd like to tell you a little bit more about myself, and Bhavesh too.

I was born in Baroda, a city in Gujarat State in India.. I have a younger sister, Chaitali, and a younger brother – Tarak. Chaitali is married with two beautiful daughters – Mahi and Krupa. I haven't been fortunate enough to spend much time with Mahi and Krupa, but by God's grace both of them have a very strong bond with us. I love them to bits. Parag and Chaitali are settled in

Canberra, Australia. My brother Tarak is married to Dhwani, and he has settled in Australia too, in Sydney.

My parents gave us the best childhood possible. They taught us lessons that have stayed with me throughout my life, and form the bedrock of my principles – giving respect to others, and the value of money. From a young age, my dad, Shahshikantbhai, embedded the virtues of hard work and discipline into us. He used to take us up into his offices, where he worked as a chartered accountant, and showed us how he took care of the family. My mum, Jayshreeben, was a housewife when we were young – and looked after us. At the time, my siblings and I just assumed that this was what she liked doing. Little did we know that she actually had a degree in economics, from Maharaja Syaji University! Now that she is all finished with her duties as a mother, she is working at my dad's office, and is doing great. Never underestimate your mum!

On top of having a wonderful family, I also have a number of close friends, starting with Aarti – who my mum loved more than me! Aarti was very studious, and a top scorer in pretty much every single subject. We studied together from nursery onwards, and to this day, we are still close. I would also like to say thank you to Rachana, her brother Niraj, Miloni, Payal, Ekta, Bhairavi and Harleen. We are not just friends, but family.

In summary:

I had the best childhood, more than I could have asked for. The people around me cared for me deeply, and made sure I was protected. I believe that this upbringing is what contributed to the bond between myself, Khushil and Bhavesh. Family is the most important thing in the world – protect it with your life.

Back row, left to right: Me (Namrata), Bhavesh, My Dad, Tarak, Dhwani, My Mum, Chaitali

Front row, left to right: Khushil, Mahi and Krupa.

February 2014

About Bhavesh

My husband, Bhavesh, was born in Ahmedabad. He has an elder sister, Neela, and a younger brother. He lives by his principles and values. Bhavesh started working at a young age, as he always wanted to be independent. His dad Gajendrabhai used to work as an accountant for Lalbhai Group (Arvind Intex). Bhavesh's mum, Hansaben, was a school teacher.

Ever since I met him, Bhavesh has been a self-sufficient and independent individual. With this in mind, he's always had business smarts. In 1991, Bhavesh decided to open his first business – selling kites. My father-in-law (Bhavesh's dad) is a firm believer in astrology, and will follow what the stars say to the nth degree. He spoke to several astrologers – all of whom told him that Bhavesh would not succeed in this business. Bhavesh did it anyway. Not only did he recover the funds needed to return the initial investment, but he also earned 66% profit. My husband is so driven that he paid for his own education, and used to work during the day and study at night. At the age when he should have been enjoying life like other children, he was working – even during Diwali time. These experiences all mean that Bhavesh understands the real value of money. After completing a degree in Law, Bhavesh has recently acquired the contract with our local council for supplying labour, and also spends time teaching computing in schools.

In terms of family, Bhavesh is just as close with his siblings as I am with mine. He is especially close with his brother. Bhavesh is the middle child, best friends with his brother, and protective of his sister and parents.

Bhavesh and I met for the first time in 1997, when I joined one of his computer classes. It was love at first sight. We'd meet before I started morning college, and then again after college. We dated for two years, and then decided to get married.

Our wedding took place on 1st April 1999. To date, we have been married for 19 years, and have also worked together in India, running our own business. Together, we have had the best time of our lives. I know it sounds very cliché but it is true. Bhavesh and I have always loved each other and taken care of each other. We have lived our lives on our own terms, and never let anyone else dictate our decisions. My in-laws made it very easy for me to get adjusted to the new family. My mother-in-law, I have always called her my mum, supported me the most. She always protected me, looked after me, and taught me lots of things. While I am talking about her, I must tell you that I didn't know how to cook at all when I got married! The only thing I knew how to make was a cup of tea. She taught me how to cook, she also taught me how to do day-to-day housework. I had no clue about any of that, as I had never had to cook or do housework at my parents' house. Unfortunately, she passed away on 24th December 2015. At this moment, I need her the most. I miss her a lot. My father-in-law has also made sure that I don't feel as if I am a new member, but as if I am the daughter of the house. Neelaben, Bhavesh's sister, is one of my greatest supporters. She has tested me, but has always made sure that I am looked after and protected. My niece, Mansi (Neelaben's daughter) was only a year-and-a-half when I got married. She is now 20-years-old. From day one she treated me as if I were her mum. Her unconditional love always made me smile, and made me feel as if I belonged to her home, as one of her family. Mansi calls me 'Tini', my pet name. She made me mum – Mansi is my first child. Ohh my GOD she is the most adorable, lovable, and cutest child! I could write a whole book on Mansi. Of course, I can't, so here's just a few of her incidents:

When she was little, Mansi never liked my parents, my brother, or my sister. My brother always used to tease her, saying, 'I am going to take your Tini'. Mansi would cry a lot and sit holding my hand the entire time while my parents visited me. She was always worried that my parents would take me away. Mansi was and still is overly possessive about me. She would choose me over anything and anyone. She always wanted me to be the best looking, no matter what. She once met someone who was very beautiful and had fair skin. She came home, took me straight up to the bedroom, and applied face powder to my hands, face and legs, saying, 'My Tini is the best.' She was so possessive that if someone sat with me or I was playing with another child then she wouldn't like it at all. In fact, that would make her angry! She would tell everyone, 'Tini is mine and I don't want anyone to come and play with her.'

In short, my in-laws are my family. I was and still am looked after by them, and for this I am incredibly grateful.

Two years after my marriage I became pregnant. Everyone was very happy, as it would be the first grandchild of my family. Obviously I was delighted – I was going to be a mum! It really was the best feeling of my life. All of a sudden, everything had changed. The people around me treated me as if I was a queen. In respect for the gift we had been given, the baby inside of me, Bhavesh decided to take a pilgrimage to Amarnath. Amarnath cave is a Hindu shrine in Jammu and Kashmir, in India. On the day that Bhavesh left for Amarnath Darsha, I found out that I had miscarried. The news was a real shock to me. I didn't know what to say or how to react. I just left the clinic and came home. After some thought, I decided that I was not going to tell Bhavesh about the miscarriage until he came back – as I didn't want him to worry whilst he was so far away from home. When he arrived back from the trip, I sat him down and broke the news. Both of us were incredibly upset, but we vowed not to let the situation take away our spirit, or impact our lives. Since that moment, we've lived true to our word. Bhavesh and I have lived in our own little world of happiness and fun. We never let any situation, however negative, take away our positive energy and attitude towards life.

As you progress through this book, you will come to understand that Bhavesh is a great man. He is a best friend to his brother, and a guardian of his sister and parents. He is the ideal son, the best dad that any child could ever have wished for, and the perfect husband. Over the past two years, our pain has been indescribable, but together we have come through it.

Khushil's Birth (Innocence)

April 2002, and I was pregnant again! We were all very happy, but very cautious at the same time. Everyone took even more care compared to my first pregnancy. I was loving every second of it, as anyone would. Everything happened almost exactly as I wanted it. We had a very grand baby shower ceremony, with a specific ritual. According to our ritual, the mum goes to her parents' home after the ceremony. I didn't really want to go, but had to follow the instructions – as that was the part of the whole baby shower ceremony. But as usual I decided what to do, and did things on my terms, so I came back after a couple of months to stay with Bhavesh. I was loved and taken care of by Bhavesh and my in-laws, to the extent that I never felt that I should just stay with my mum during the last days of my pregnancy. I stayed with Bhavesh for a few weeks, and then went back to my mum's house. I was obviously loved and spoilt there too!

Then came the big day – 8th December 2002. My handsome son was born at 4am. My first child, no words could express my joy and happiness. In our religion, 4am is Brahm Muhrat – which is the time when all the Gods take a bath. It's considered a very auspicious time. My mum was with me, so she called my dad and Bhavesh to hospital and gave them the good news. Everyone was very happy, Khushil was the first grandchild from my parent's family, and the second grandchild in Bhavesh family. Now, we had to think of a name. We looked at lots of names, but none of them felt right. Finally, we narrowed it down to two choices – Khush (meaning happy person) and Khushil (meaning happiness, who gives happiness to all). We liked Khushil, and so this was the name given to my adorable, cute, little son. As his name suggested, he was giving everyone happiness!

I was the first one to have a baby in my friendship group. Khushil was loved and pampered by both his grandparents. For my sister and brother, and my friends, he was like their first child. He was everyone's favourite. As soon as my dad came home from the office every day that would be it – he'd take Khushil and no one else would get chance to play with him! Tarak, my brother, used to teach Khushil all the naughty stuff – like how to tear newspaper while my dad was reading it.

Khushil with his grandparents, celebrating his 3rd birthday, 2005

From birth, Khushil had something special about him. I could feel it even before he was born. As a baby, he gave everyone a chance to enjoy and live their childhood again. His innocent and adorable smile infatuated everyone. Experiencing the innocence of Khushil was inexpressible. His eyes were mesmerising and his smile gracious. He gave me the most respectable title on earth – Mum. I was reborn on 8th December 2002. My world had changed in a moment. I don't know how, but instantly everything was different. Khushil and I had the most special bond, from the very moment he was born. I couldn't let him go even for a second, I couldn't have him out of my sight. Bhavesh was extremely happy to hold him, he couldn't believe that he was holding his first child. Khushil meant the world to both of us. All we wanted was for Khushil to live a healthy life and to achieve his goals. We wanted to protect him, as parents, but at the same time we were his best friends.

Khushil at three-years-old, with his teddy

On the 19th of December, just eleven days after Khushil's birth, we had saints from Swaminarayan temple visit us – to give Khushil blessings. It is very rare that the saints pay home visits for blessings to a newborn. As per the tradition, women don't visit the saints. Khushil was wrapped in my silk sari. As soon as they saw him the first words that they said were, 'He is a mukt jev' (exonerated). Khushil played with them for a couple of hours.

To describe Khushil is not easy. He had a very special quality to him, almost an aura of some kind. He was soft hearted, but his personality was so strong. This might seem like a contradiction, and you might be wondering how someone can be both of those things. By the end of this book I hope to explain to you and justify why this was, and I'm confident that you too will be able to vouch for it.

Khushil attracted everyone that came in touch with him. Vegetable and fruit vendors used to come to my home and take Khushil with them, and bring him back when they were returning from work. They used to love him and liked playing with him while doing their work. They treated him with fruits and vegetables. Khushil used to come home happy, nearly always carrying some treat or other in his hands. In those days, we had a cleaner, who used to take Khushil out after dinner every day for a walk, and then used to take him to play with his friends. Sometimes I had to go searching for Khushil, because everyone in the neighbourhood loved having him at their houses!

Khushil's sleeping time was a special time, as it always

is for babies. I used to sing him Smaranjalika (devotional songs) to make him sleep. He loved listening to them. For the first year Khushil didn't sleep at night. He would sleep during the day and evening time. He would wake up at 10pm and then go to sleep at 5.30am early morning. He played all the time, and never cried. Since I didn't get the chance to play with him during the day, night time was our special mother and son time. I can still picture him as a sleeping baby, absolutely adorable, with a hypnotising smile.

In 2003, Bhavesh decided to apply for a United Kingdom visa. He got the visa in October 2003, and came to the UK on 25th September 2003. Khushil was just 10-months-old. On Khushil's first birthday Bhavesh was not with us, but he insisted that we celebrate Khushil's birthday anyway, and we did. Everyone enjoyed the celebrations, but my eyes kept on looking for Bhavesh. We had never stayed that far away from each other. Ultimately, Bhavesh didn't like it here (London) without us, so he came back to India in January.

While Bhavesh was in India, he had taken Khushil to a temple where we had Pramukh Swami Maharaj, in Ahmedabad. The Swami was present in the temple Sabha, and was going to give blessings to everyone present. Pramukh Swaminaraya Maharah was the Guru and President of the BAPS Swaminarayan Sanstha. Under his presidency Swami had overseen the growth of the organisation, centred in Gujarat, India, spread around the world. Under his presidency the organisation has held a wide range of community charity projects, and have received many awards – including a

Guinness World Record. He is a very respectable and spiritual Guru. That day, there were hundreds of people visiting the temple. Everyone queued up, and one by one people started to receive their blessings. In this crowd of hundreds, Khushil was lucky, as the Swami called Bhavesh over and touched Khushil's forehead. This was very rare – Swami's don't touch everyone, and rarely single people out, so only the lucky few get their blessings this way.

Over the next few years Khushil met different Swamis a few times, and every time he met them they all said that he was a mukt jev (exonerated). At that point I was not sure what they were trying to tell me, but I was of course happy that he was getting blessings every time, and that they were praising him! As a mum what more could I ask for?

Khushil playing with starfish, Brighton beach, aged 2

Bhavesh decided that he was not going to come back to London, but all our family and friends encouraged him to try once again, and offered telephone support if he needed it. With this in mind, Bhavesh eventually decided to give it another go, and returned to London in March. I then applied for a visa for Khushil and myself – which we received in March. Everyone was telling me that I should leave Khushil, and that they would take care of him. They said that I should take him to London once we had settled. Bhavesh and I were absolutely firm that if I went to London then Khushil had to be with me. I was not ready to leave him. I wanted to be with him at every stage, and see him grow up. I wanted to be the first person to hear him speak, to see him walk, to see him become a man.

Khushil, 3-years-old

I wanted to be the first person he recognised. As a mum, how could I possibly miss these events? So, I came with Khushil to London on the 7th May 2004. I must say that Bhavesh, Khushil and I were extremely happy. I think that moving to London was almost like a rebirth for the three of us. It was fresh and exciting, and we all enjoyed the change of scenery.

Obviously, we had some adapting to do. We wanted to try and see if we are all comfortable. It was a new country, a new culture, and a completely different environment. I studied English back in India, but it was still a different accent and brought a variety of new challenges. We always had a belief though, that as long as we were together, then we could be successful. Bhavesh already had a job working for Royal Mail. So, Khushil and I enjoyed our first few months, just sitting at home and chilling.

In India, Bhavesh had his own business – which involved gaining contracts for teaching computing in schools. We had teachers on our payroll, who would then go into schools and teach. When Bhavesh came to England, I was running the business on my own, on top of teaching at school in the mornings, when Khushil was sleeping. I used to finish my school teaching at 12.30, and then come home and take care of the business side of things.

I had never done a paid job before that point, I always worked for myself. I was always a businesswoman. The first challenge was to actually find a job. The second, most difficult part, was to actually gain employment. It was a big step for me. I had never envisioned myself working for someone else, and I had never experienced having to answer to someone or having a manager. It felt so alien to me. However, I did find a job in the Royal Mail post office, as a cashier. So, both Bhavesh and I were employed by the same company.

Bhavesh worked full-time, and I worked part-time. Now that we both had a job, we had to find a child minder to look after Khushil. I was again very firm that I wouldn't leave Khushil with just anyone. I would only leave Khushil with someone once I was satisfied and had the confirmation that Khushil would be looked after.

Khushil in Goa, during Diwali, 2005

When searching for someone to look after Khushil, we went to see lots of different childminders' houses, but I just didn't like any of them. I just never got the feeling that I could leave Khushil there and feel satisfied in the knowledge he was being looked after. Let's call it a mother's instinct. Then, one day, I met Shantaba. She called me over and said, 'I remember your son and his pushchair.' I was extremely confused at this point, and wondering how exactly she knew me.

Then she said, 'I was on the same flight as you, as I was visiting my sister in India.' She remembered Khushil, and she said, 'I kept on thinking that he is such an adorable child and he is so well behaved.' She remembered his pushchair and also the photos that we were taking outside the airport. From that day on, we had an extremely close relationship. I felt as if I had someone who I could really rely on. Even then though, it was so hard leaving Khushil. I had never left him with anyone else apart from my family, so dropping him off with Shantaba, as much as I trusted her, filled me with anguish.

Every day, as soon as I came to pick Khushil up, he would hug me. Reuniting with Khushil, even after just a few hours, was magical. It was unforgettable. Even while writing this I feel his love, his smile, and his hug, all of which meant the world to me. I wanted to work hard for my son, to give him the best childhood and life possible. Khushil being Khushil, he won everyone's heart at Shantaba's home, and was very popular with her neighbours and family members. They treated him like a prince. As an example, nobody was even allowed to change the television channel without Khushil's permission!

His place where he sat in the living room was fixed, and he even had a special pillow and a duvet in Shantaba's house. She would cook him whatever he asked for, and get dinner ready for when he went to sleep. Not only that, but if she made something that Khushil loved over the weekend, then she would make sure that she saved some for Khushil's visit on Monday. In short, Khushil was treated like Shantaba's grandchild, and he absolutely loved going to her house. As a mum, I felt satisfied that he was safe and enjoying himself.

While we are talking about Khushil's childhood, let me tell you about a particular incident, which occurred when we visited Buckingham Palace. My in-laws had come to visit us, so we decided to go and see somewhere famous and historical. It was a very lovely sunny day. We all got our tickets and entered into the Palace.

I have to say that from the inside, Buckingham Palace is breathtaking. Each and everything is carefully and minutely designed to perfection. There are gold plated railings on the stairs, and the painting, decoration and interior are spectacular. It's enough to make you want to experience royal life. When we visited there, Khushil was still very young – just 5 years old. He was just walking around, looking at all the enormous rooms. Then, we all entered one room, and suddenly Khushil was extremely interested. He was very curious to touch one of the chairs. The room in question was the room in which the Queen would pass on the throne to her successor. Before I could stop him, Khushil decided to go underneath the barrier and sit on the chair that was for the successor! Obviously I couldn't follow him, as we were not allowed to go in. The guard followed him and brought him back to me. The guard was very nice, and he calmly managed the situation and brought Khushil down from the chair in a friendly manner. He then told me, 'Your son has a very royal taste.'

I didn't know at that point that Khushil was a real king, and was going to rule over so many hearts. I didn't know how much love and respect he would earn in his life that I would be writing a book about him, with all you lovely readers following with interest. I am a very proud mum. In this book I want to show you that every child is extraordinary and special, and that every child has very special and unique qualities. Given the chance, they will do their very best to make you a proud parent.

Khushil in Egypt, 2015

Life was treating us with love, and we felt as if there was an angel looking after us. Come February 2013, Khushil was now eleven. We are Hindu Brahmin, so we had to do Yajnopavit Samskaras (thread ceremony) for Khushil. The ceremony is normally performed at the age of nine, eleven, or thirteen. It is one of the traditional

Samskaras that marks the acceptance of a student by a Guru, and an individual student entrance to a school. In ancient India, students used to go to Gurukuls for studies. Hence it is that age, as before, that they study at home. Then, when they become independent, they are send to Gurukul – away from home – for studies.

We decided to do the Yajnopavit Samskaras for Khushil at the age of eleven, as we wanted to make sure that he understood the whole ceremony, and enjoyed the rituals. In our culture this is four-day ceremony, where we welcome our Kuldevi (family deity goddess) to give us blessings and protect us from any disturbance that could occur during the Pooja. On the first and the second day we perform Ganesh Pooja, Mandap Mahurat, in which Lord Ganesh is worshipped, and pray to him to remove all the obstacles, and we also perform Aarti during the morning and evening time. The third day is a big day, which starts with the Ganesh Staphana, as we always do Pooja of Ganesh before we start any ceremony, followed by the Pithi Ceremony – which is an auspicious ritual performed for good luck. After that, Mundan (shaving the head) is done, before the child wears the Sacred Thread.

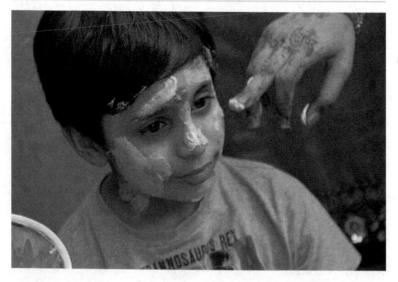

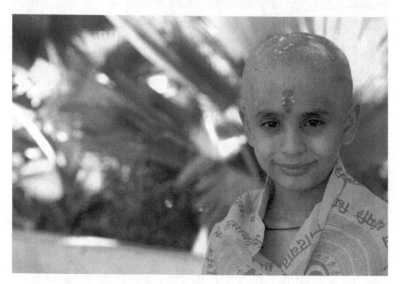

Khushil's Janoy Ceremony, 2013

Nowadays, Mundan has become very uncommon. It is a part of the Janoy which has been forgotten. So, not all the kids get it done. We had discussed it with Khushil before the ceremony, and he was happy to go through with it. He said, 'I believe in that, and I will get it done.' The priest was pleasantly surprised by this. He said to us, 'I have done eleven Janoys this year, and Khushil is the first boy who has done Mundan. I am impressed, boys living in India are not getting it done.'

The Sacred Thread has symbolic meaning, and has three strands. The three strands of the thread symbolise three debts of man which must never be forgotten: the debt of the teacher, the debt of the parents, and the debt of the ancestors, including scholars. The Sacred Thread is also the symbol of the three goddesses: Parvati, Lakshmi, and Saraswati. A person becomes complete only with the help of these three deities of strength, wealth, and knowledge respectively.

After the child wears the Scared Thread, the Priest teaches the Gayatri Mantra

ॐ भूर्भुवः स्वः ।तत्सवितुर्वरेण्यं भर्गो देवस्यधीमहि। धियो यो नः प्रचोदयात् ॥

Meaning

"We meditate on the glory of that Being who has produced this universe; may He enlighten our minds." As per the translation done by Swami Vivekananda.

Following this, the priest then puts a few things onto a plate: a pen, money, Shri Bhagwat Gita, a mirror and a pair of scissors. The child is then given an explanation about the significance of each of the items kept, and then given a chance to choose one of the items. It is believed that the item chosen will give a hint as to the future for the child. Khushil picked up a pen, which is the symbol of education. The pen is an indication that the chooser will study and earn fame in the world of education.

On the last day, we say goodbye to our Kuldevi (we call it Mataji Vadavana) and ask for blessings that we will have another child, another opportunity to hold another ceremony, to which we can invite everyone.

The entire ceremony is celebrated for 4 days, and all close family and friends are invited for lunch and dinner. The third day is the biggest day, and on that day all family and friends, extended family members and neighbours are invited to take part in the ceremony and give blessings to the boy. We invited roughly 500 guests to take part in the ceremony on day 3.

Khushil's Janoy Ceremony, 2013

Naturally, Khushil absolutely loved all of this. Since the whole ceremony was for him, everyone looked after him, and he received lots of gifts. When Bhavesh and I asked him about what gift he wanted for us, he instantly said, 'I want a book.' He selected *The Encyclopaedia of Animals: The Complete Visual Guide*. Books were the one thing that he was always interested in, and he would always be happy to get one. Whilst he was enjoying himself, he also embraced all of the individual facets of the ceremony. He respected each and every Pooja, and performed them with the utmost belief. He respected the Sacred Thread, and wore it all the time. He also made sure that he did the Gayatri Mantra every day, just as anyone who wears Janeu is meant to.

This was the one ceremony that I was very excited about, as I was equally involved, and both Khushil and I had the opportunity to perform the rituals. Thanks Khushil, for giving me the opportunity. My sister and brother had come from Australia, and Bhavesh's two brothers had come from the USA and Canada. This was the first time that all our brothers and sisters and cousins who had left India to settle in different countries were going to meet. In fact, we were all going to meet together for the first time. It was very exciting to be a part of the ceremony, and meet our full and extended family.

Overall, February 2013 was an amazing month. Bhavesh's Granddad had his ninetieth birthday on 2nd Feb, then it was Rupal's ninth birthday, my maternal uncle's eleventh wedding anniversary, and Tarak's engagement on the 12th. On the 14th we had Bhavikbhai's wedding, and her birthday the very next day. For the week beginning the 17th we had Khushil's Janeu, and finally on the 22nd it was Neelaben's wedding anniversary. It was a month of love and celebration.

Khushil at his Janoy evening ceremony, reading a book, 2013

Life In London

Moving to London was a scary time for the three of us. I must say that although we welcomed the new start, we were very worried about how we would manage in a new country. We had so many questions, and so few answers. Where would we work? What would we do if it went wrong? Would my experience and qualifications be taken into account when applying for a job? As you can imagine, changing city or state is hard enough, but we'd gone one step further. It was a new country, a new environment and a new culture. Most importantly, it was just the 3 of us.

To my surprise, we were welcomed with open arms by the people of London. We made new friends, who have now become family to us. The very first lovely couple that we met in London were Mr & Mrs Karia, then Mr & Mrs Shah, and then Shantaba, Jayantidada, Priya, Manish and Sapna. Shantaba and her family have a very special place in our life, and are our parents away from home.

As they say, God always has better plans for us. After Shantaba we met a lot of beautiful and good-hearted people, and they too have become part of our family. Some we had already known from back in India, and some we met here for the first time. To name a few: Mrs Vaghela and her family. Himanshubhai, Purvibhabhi, Astha, Priyanshi, Minal, Zankar, Krisha, Zia, Dipu, Anjali, Shaurya, Jalpaben and her parents, Hem, Perry, Chintabhai and his family, Bhaveshbhai and his family, Ankurbhai, Kalpnaben and her family, Binjalben and her family (Ben is used to pay respect to a women and Bhai for men). Not only have we made good friends outside of work, but at work as well – such as Hayley, Des, Kelly, Richard, Sajida, Yusuf, Sangita, Dele, and many more. I could write a whole book of names, but don't worry I have no plans to do that!

Hayley has been extremely supportive to me through the most difficult part of my life. In truth, all my family, friends, and work colleagues have played a very important role in helping me get through a very tough journey. You will see their names again in the latter part of this book. There will be a few other names that you will see again too.

I must say, life has always treated us well. There is definitely someone who is looking after Bhavesh and I. Through my experiences in London, I have learned an awful lot. I have gained more self-confidence, and most importantly, I have found my identity. Before I came to this city, I was Shashikantbhai's daughter, and then Bhavesh's wife – never Namrata. Now, I know who I am, and I am proud to be me.

Khushil at Weymouth Beach, 2006, aged 4

Khushil and His School

Khushil's love for his school was phenomenal. It is said that school serves as a child's second home, but for Khushil it was his first home. He loved going to school, and studying was his passion. From a very young age he had decided that he wanted to become a scientist. His dream was to become a zoologist, and research, with the aim of increasing the longevity of certain species of animals – namely those that were on the verge of extinction. He was very affectionate, compassionately caring for all types of animals, bugs, and sea creatures.

Khushil went to nursery, and then juniors, at Roe Green Junior School. I can still remember his first day of school. I went to drop him off at school, and because it was the first day parents were allowed to stay with the kids. He kept on telling me, 'Go home, I am fine, go.' He forced me to leave the school. I did as he asked, but of course, being his mum, I waited outside the gates. It was so emotional that I sat outside crying, it was a very mixed feeling. I was very worried to leave him, with completely new people and kids that he had never met. I was worried about whether he'd be able to adjust, and whether he'd be safe or looked after. My heart was beating very fast, and I was feeling very nervous and anxious about everything. Every minute felt like an hour. I am sure that any parents reading this will be able to relate to their child's first day of school.

Khushil with Namrata, aged 3

Finally, it was time to pick Khushil up. I went in and hugged him straight away. I know kids don't like this in front of other students, but I couldn't control it. It made Khushil feel awkward, but Khushil being Khushil, he just looked at me and gave me a hug back. He smiled, and that smile made me forget the time that I had waited outside the school worrying about him. I was extremely happy to see him, and he looked very happy to have completed his first day at school.

Some children hate school, some love it. I think Khushil's love for school was somewhat unusual, but in a way that I am deeply proud of. I don't remember a day when he said, 'I don't want to go to school today.' He would never let me book a day off school. Even if we were going on holiday, and the holiday fell one day before the summer holidays started, there was no chance. School was always his priority, and he would never let anything get in the way of his studies.

Khushil was always extremely organised for one so young. He had a tight schedule, and he kept to it. As soon as he came home from school, he'd have his shower immediately – regardless of the weather. Then, from 1600 till 1630 he would eat his dinner, and watch cartoons. From 1630 onwards was his own time. He called this 'my time' and usually spent this playing console games, whether it was on the Xbox, PlayStation, PSP or iPad. We allocated an hour for this. We never had to tell him that his hour was up, he would just finish playing on the dot. If he needed any extra time for the game, then he would always ask for permission. From 17:30 till 18:30 was his creativity time. He loved drawing, and watching animal shows – he was particularly fond of Steve Backshall and "Deadly 60", along with David Attenborough.

I had always loved watching TV with Khushil. He would sit next to me, leaning on me and cuddling me, and I also ended up learning a lot from the TV shows that he was watching! Originally, we started by telling Khushil that you can only play your game for an hour, and then you have to study, and then you can watch television. But Khushil being Khushil, we never had to tell him anything twice. He would always obey, and do what he was told. He was the most obedient child I have ever seen. He was a dream child, and will always remain a dream child for me.

When he started school, Khushil didn't talk to anyone.

He would only talk to one teacher, Mrs Parekh. This was because Gujarati was our first language, and we talked Gujarati at home. So, Khushil was not confident talking in English. He definitely picked up the English language very quickly, but was still very shy, so he wouldn't talk to all of his classmates. In Year 5 when I went for a parents' meeting, his English teacher told me that Khushil has progressed phenomenally.

Normally the students take two terms to reach the level that Khushil has achieved in two months. His teachers also used to say that he had a very cute face and a mesmerising smile.

As I've already mentioned, Khushil was highly selective about whom he spoke to and made friends with. He was a very particular child, and very precise on where his things should be kept. At school, when it came to tidy-up time, he would make sure that the things were kept in exactly the right place, so they could be picked up for playing. His teachers told me that he would not appreciate someone else putting his toys in a different place, and if they did then he would have to go and make sure they were placed correctly. Khushil was so precise in his work that when he came back from school he would keep his school bag and lunch box in a special space in the kitchen, which he had created especially for this. He had a special place in his heart for his school bag, as he loved school, and had respect for education from the beginning. Never once did I hear any complaint from teachers or the school about Khushil being disrespectful, quite the opposite in fact.

I can still remember one particular Saturday, when

Bhavesh rang me and then gave the phone to Khushil. He said hello, in his innocent and cute voice, and then for the first time he recited the alphabet – from A to Z. We had been teaching him five letters at a time. In ten days, he had learnt the entire thing. I was extremely happy, and even today I can still hear his soft voice saying, 'Mum, I have said the whole ABCD, are you happy?' I was the proudest mum in the world. I bet all parents can remember their child's first word, their first smile, when they walked for the first time, their first teeth, their first day at school, and every other first that you could imagine. Every child stays a child for their parents.

Khushil was genuinely unique, and had the ability and willingness to be the best in all areas, with the humblest attitude and a very down-to-earth approach to his success. Just to give you an example, Khushil had a fellow classmate who was a little short tempered. He had physically beaten Khushil a few times at school, and there was one occasion when he really took it too far. I was lucky that my family friend was in school, and she saved Khushil. This fellow classmate was sitting on the top of Khushil and hitting him!

As any mum would be, I was fuming, and was extremely worried. I couldn't stop crying when they told me what had happened. Please don't get me wrong here, I am not criticising anyone, just trying to give you an example of how Khushil looked at things with a completely different view and attitude. He was only year 3 at the time. When we questioned him about the incident, Khushil just said, 'It's his (classmate's) way of getting his anger out. I am not like that. I cannot change myself and be rough and

51

disobey school rules.' His response was remarkably wise and thoughtful, and clearly shows that age doesn't define maturity.

I once read a quote that said, "Maturity is when you have the power to answer someone who did you wrong, but you just breathe and walk away and let life take care of them." Khushil is the perfect example of this. He always believed that integrity is everything. He tried lifting others up, emotionally, and this was how he showed his strength.

As I have mentioned, Khushil's enthusiasm for school had no bounds. His school projects were always kept by his teachers until the end of the year, and were then put on display. These projects included making a miniature cardboard school, a wooden plane, a science project researching the Solar System, and a history project on Egypt. We all did the latter one together, as Khushil wanted to make himself an ancient tomb. We'd just bought him a bike, so he decided to use the box that it came in to build his tomb. He found a picture of exactly how it should look, painted it in gold and brown, and then made a mummy. We stuck together some of my jewellery boxes, some plastic utensils, and some of Khushil's super hero figures too, as he wanted to be buried with them! Then, using Khushil's special book on Egyptian language and history, we wrote Tutankhamun on the tomb in gold glittery letters, in both Egyptian and English. It took us 4 days, and by the time we had finished I was exhausted! Khushil had extremely high standards for work, to the point where it was hard for us to stick to this sometimes. When it came to the project on the Solar System, Khushil would spend all of his time researching. He'd watch the Discovery Channel, and make us buy him books, just so he could learn every single thing possible – and complete the project to the highest possible level. The year when Khushil had a project on the Solar System, we went to Florida for our summer holidays. Khushil had selected to go to NASA, and was happy that he would have one day less to spend in Disney Land.

In life, it's very easy to lose focus and deviate from your goal. But with Khushil this was never an issue.

He knew exactly what he wanted to do when he grew up – working as a zoologist. He knew that he had to study very hard for this though, to be the best at what he wanted to do. His love for animals, and wanting to become a zoologist, was just another example of how Khushil always desired to bring a positive change to the world.

Khushil would pretty much read any book that contained information about animals, reptiles, or sea creatures. He had detailed information about almost every species, such as their habitat, what they ate, how long they lived, and how many of them there were in the world. He had an incredible ability to retain all the knowledge that he had gained by reading books. On top of knowledge-based books, he also read lots of Anthony Horowitz, and Steve Backshall. Possibly his favourite book was written by Dynamo, titled *Nothing Is Impossible.* Books were one of the most important parts of his life, and there was never a day when he wasn't reading for at least an hour. Whenever we went on holiday Khushil would buy a book, then when we got on the plane we would read the book for the entire journey. On the way back, we'd buy him another book, and he'd do the same. Sometimes he'd become so engrossed in the book that he wouldn't even ask for food or water!

Another thing about Khushil was that he only read physical books. He would absolutely not read eBooks – the book had to be a physical copy for him. He would look after his physical books as if they were jewels, and he'd never ever give them away. Once Khushil read a book he would keep it forever. We still have all of his old books.

Khushil studied until year 6 in Roe Green Junior School. From year 7 he went to Claremont High School. Khushil sat for his 11+ exams, but took a different route to his friends. All of his friends from junior school naturally progressed on to Kingsbury High School. But, again, and you will see me repeat these words many times throughout the course of this book, Khushil being Khushil he decided to go to an open evening at Claremont High School. He loved Claremont's presentation, the way the whole evening was conducted, and the lovely students who showed us round the school. Khushil requested to visit almost every part of the school that evening. The highlight, which pretty much sealed the deal for Khushil, was the science laboratory. He absolutely loved it. On top of this, we were very near to the school, so this increased Khushil's chances of admission.

As per Khushil's instructions, we informed Roe Green School that Khushil had decided to join Claremont, following the end of year 6. The majority of schools have two trial days for students, prior to the end of year 6, where they'll spend time in the new school. These two days were very important for Khushil, as he wanted to make sure that he had made the right decision. I am not saying that it was just his decision, of course Bhavesh and I had a say, but Khushil's view naturally carried more weight. In any case, he loved the two days that he spent at Claremont, and came home telling us that the school was amazing, that the teachers were excellent, and that the students were all extremely helpful if he got lost.

Khushil's last day at Roe Green was on the 24th July 2014. I cannot forget that day. It was a day of mixed emotions. Khushil was happy to join his new school, but at the same time it was the last day he would be spending with his close friends. They all had a fantastic day – signing a leaving book, writing messages, and signing a school t-shirt. The school gave all of the students a lovely gift – the Roe Green Autograph book, in which they wrote lovely messages. At the end of the day all of the students had a party, including the teachers. They had an ice-cream, and then the kids decided to play football.

While they were playing football, Khushil decided to use his skills and try a bicycle kick. The kick didn't go as planned. Instead he slipped and landed on his right hand, which caused a fracture in his elbow. It was extremely painful. The school rang me immediately. Naturally I was very scared and worried. Millions of thoughts were going through my mind, and not good ones either. Like any mum, I was all panicky, and I felt as if my heart was going to stop.

I was very far from the school and would not have been able to get there for at least an hour. So, I rang Shantaba. She was out shopping, but she left all her shopping and went straight to the school, picked up Khushil and called the ambulance to take him to the hospital. He was in so much pain that it was not possible for Shantaba to take him to the hospital in her car. She started praying for the ambulance to arrive quickly, and was in tears, as she couldn't bear to see Khushil like that. Meanwhile, I was losing my mind, trying to reach Khushil as quickly as possible. I had a brain freeze, and just couldn't think properly. I don't even remember how I managed to reach home and then the hospital.

As soon as I saw Khushil, I felt the pain that he was going through, but I must say that I had peace of mind knowing that Shantaba was with him, and that he had been well looked after. Since birth, Khushil had always needed me when he was not feeling well. He wouldn't let the doctors do the X-Ray until I had reached him. He wanted me next to him, and wouldn't let anyone touch his arm. But even with that immense pain, he was so brave.

Bhavesh and I reached the hospital about an hour after Khushil arrived. After that we went to get his X-Ray. and then he was taken for his operation. By the time he was taken for the operation it was 2200. Khushil had been in the hospital since 1630, and had not had anything to eat or drink since 1500. The nurses did ask him a few times, 'Are you okay?' but he always just had one answer, 'I am fine.' All he was worried about was the t-shirt he was wearing, which had been signed by his friends. He kept asking for it to be taken off or cut in a way that all the signatures were safe.

Khushil asked for me to be in the operation theatre with him, so in I went, mouth mask and apron fully equipped. Then, once the anaesthesia was administered, I went out. After the operation Khushil was taken to the recovery room, where he slowly gained consciousness. He hadn't eaten for a long time, and was so hungry that it affected his breathing – meaning the staff wouldn't shift him to a different room so he could eat. By that point it was roughly 1230 at night. At last, at quarter to one in the morning, we were shifted and Khushil got to eat. As soon as he saw Bhavesh, the first thing he said was, 'Bhavesh, I did not cry.' We both smiled, and felt extremely proud of our brave son. Khushil was admitted for two days in total. After that, we had a doctor visit every week, and after four weeks Khushil had his plaster removed, plus some physiotherapy treatment, along with basic exercises at home. This is how we spent the entire summer holidays of year 6!

Roe Green was fantastic for Khushil, and he grew hugely in terms of confidence. He made some great friends and had some incredible memories. A special mention must go to Ms Lehane, Ms Safi, Ms Butcher and Mr Cook, all of whom Khushil was particularly fond of.

Now, it was time to enter a new world – Claremont High School.

Claremont High School
(Khushil's First Home)

On the 4th September 2014, we dropped Khushil off for his first day at Claremont. I was extremely worried, because he still had not fully recovered from his injury. We left him at the assembly hall. I kept trying to peep into the hall, to see where he was sitting. Whilst I was doing this, the executive headteacher Mr Molloy passed me by, took me inside the hall, and showed me where Khushil was sitting. He said, in a very calm and reassuring voice, 'He is safe.' I told him that Khushil had an injury and had not fully recovered, to which Mr Molloy assured me that Khushil would be fine and taken care of.

Claremont was an extremely important stage in Khushil's life. With this in mind, this chapter has two parts to it. In the first part of this chapter, I will tell you some of the experiences that Khushil had, and in the second part I will demonstrate the amazing relationship that Khushil had with those at the school. More than that, this chapter is where you can begin to stretch your imagination, and really start to find your own sense of perception.

In year 7, Khushil was placed in set 2 for Maths. He was not happy with this, as he'd always been in set 1 for Maths at Roe Green. Consequently, he worked extremely hard to get the highest marks possible in all of the tests that he was set – he wanted to be moved to set 1 by the end of the year, or at the first opportunity provided.

We had our first parents' evening in December. As always, Khushil was very particular, and stressed the importance of what Bhavesh and I wore. He wanted us to look our absolute best. I let him decide my dress, what shoes I wore, and even which handbag I took. It was important for Khushil that we made the right impression.

I was very excited for the evening, as I would get to meet all the teachers and receive an update on Khushil's progress. All of the teachers were very happy with Khushil's behaviour, his attitude towards study, and his progress. His Maths teacher told me that Khushil was ready for set 1. This made our evening, and the rest went as expected. We went out for dinner to celebrate his success. My in-laws were here in London, as they had come to celebrate Diwali that year. They were very proud of Khushil and were happy to hear about his progress. At that moment, it felt like life was perfect, and I couldn't ask for anything more than what I had.

My in-laws then returned to India on the 14th December. After my in-laws returned to India, we noticed that Khushil had a squint in his eye, but then when he blinked a few times it was fine. Again, at the end of January 2015 we noticed the same squint, but again he blinked a few times and it was fine. Naturally, we paid no attention to it, and got back to our day-to-day life.

Khushil wanted to go on holiday for February half-term. All of our holiday destinations were always selected by Khushil. He had thought about them carefully, and was very picky in selecting the destination. It wasn't that he would just pick any place, it had to have special significance. This time, he wanted to go to Egypt. He wanted to see the pyramids and the ancient tombs. So, off we went! It was a fantastic trip. We stayed in Sharm-el-Sheikh, and visited locations such as the Temple of Karnak, the Valley of Kings, Luxor Temple, the Temple of Hatshepsut, the Colossi of Memnon, Luxor Museum and the Tomb of King Tutankhamun.

Khushil in Egypt. February 2015

At this point, I would like to share with you a quote:

"Don't worry too much about the past, as it is gone. We don't know anything about the future, so why worry? Enjoy your today, which is rightly called the present."

We returned from Egypt very happy. We'd had an amazing holiday, and spent some lovely time together as a family. After we came back, Khushil said, 'Why don't we go to India in the Easter holidays, and surprise my grandparents?' We booked the tickets for the second week of March.

Now, suddenly, the squint in Khushil's left eye had reappeared. This time the eye stayed squinted, even when he blinked. Khushil wanted it to be checked here, in England, but I asked him whether it would be ok if we got it checked in India. He was adamant that he wanted it checked before we travelled. So, we booked an appointment with the eye optician on Kingsbury High road.

The appointment was booked for the 24th March 2015, after school. On that day, as usual, I woke up at six in the morning, got ready, did my Pooja, then made myself a cup of tea. While I was boiling my tea I prepared Khushil's lunch for school, and made breakfast for Bhavesh and Khushil. I had also prepared Khushil's favourite pasta for him to eat when he got back from school.

Khushil was extremely punctual and fussy about getting to school on time. He had never once been late. So, I woke up him up at 7:30am as normal, kissed him goodbye at 8am, then left for work. I was completely unaware that this day, 24th March 2015, would throw our whole lives out of orbit.

Khushil's eye appointment was at 16:30. I left work an hour early, called Khushil, and asked him to come and meet me at Kingsbury Station. At 16:20 I reached Kingsbury station. Khushil being Khushil, he was punctual, and had already arrived. We walked to the opticians. After a short wait, the doctor examined Khushil, and then immediately told us that we should visit the Western Eye Hospital. I rang Bhavesh, and told him that we were going to the hospital. We arrived at the hospital at 17:45.

Since we were going for a walk-in, we faced a long wait at the hospital. We waited for nearly two hours before Bhavesh arrived, and then we were called in to see the doctor. Initially, the doctor did a few checks, then she called in another doctor who did the same checks. I was confused and didn't understand what was going on. I asked the doctor, 'Is everything okay?' The doctor replied, 'Don't know, Mum, I can't say for sure. Which is your nearest hospital?' To this, I said, 'Northwick Park.'

The doctor rang Northwick Park hospital and then told us that we should go straight there, and that they would admit Khushil and perform an MRI scan tomorrow. By that time, it was 21:00. We had to go back home to get the car, so we went home and had dinner, before leaving to go to the hospital. We still didn't know what was going on, and as you can imagine we were very worried.

When we reached the hospital, the medical staff were waiting for us. The doctor informed me that they would do an MRI scan the following morning. I asked him, 'Is there anything to worry about?' and he said, 'No, it's just a routine check-up to find the reason for the squint.' Deep inside, Bhavesh and I were extremely scared, and wondering whether Khushil would have problems with vision for the rest of his life, and other such horrible thoughts. I couldn't sleep the whole night, I just kept on looking at Khushil and thinking about all the possibilities, and the worst-case scenarios. I prayed to God that it would be okay.

At 6am the next day, I texted Hayley, to tell her that I

was at the hospital and wouldn't be able to come in. Bhavesh arrived at the hospital at 7am, and stayed with Khushil whilst I went home and got ready, and then I came back to the hospital at 8:30am. Khushil was taken for his MIR at 10am. I went in with him and sat next to him throughout the scan. This was the first time I had seen an MRI machine. It was massive, and I was uncomfortable at the thought of Khushil having to go inside of it. I was scared of the whole process. The machine made an enormous noise. Khushil and I were given headphones to cover our ears. Khushil was told to stay still through the whole process, because if he moved then it would mean that they would have to carry out the scan again. The scan took thirty minutes, and I was saying the Gayatri Mantra while I was sitting with him. After the scan, my heart had a weird feeling, as if something bad was going to happen.

We were told that we would be given the result by 13:00. At about 11am we decided to take Khushil to the canteen so that he could have a drink and something to eat. Each and every minute felt like an hour.

While I am writing this, I am living the moments again. I can feel the restlessness and curiosity. I can feel the butterflies in my stomach. There was so much going through my mind, and I couldn't concentrate. There was this strange, scared feeling, unexplainable, but at the same time my face was showing my worry. I am not sure if everyone would have noticed, but Khushil surely noticed it. Khushil and Bhavesh had something to eat, and then we came back up. At 12:30 a doctor came and told us that she would like to see us in a separate room, to discuss the results of the scan.

A nurse sat with Khushil talking to him about his school, whilst Bhavesh and I spoke to Dr Afif. I was concerned, and was not entirely sure what was going on. My heart had started beating fast. My hands and feet had gone cold. I had a terrible, indescribable feeling in my stomach.

The first question that Dr Afif asked was, 'Is Khushil an only child?'

After a little pause, I replied, 'Yes, why?'

Dr Afif said, 'I would like you both to listen to me carefully and patiently. The scan results show that your son has a brain tumour. We have sent the MRI scan to UCLH (University College London Hospitals), and the doctors have confirmed that it is cancerous.

Now, the next step is for you to have an appointment with the doctor at UCLH. Khushil will be admitted here for a week, and then shifted to UCLH. We are waiting to hear from the doctor to give us a line of action to be taken. All they have told us at the moment is that Khushil needs to be put on Dexamethasone (steroids).'

There was a short pause, whilst we took everything in. Then Dr Afif said, 'Do you have any questions? Did you understand what I explained to you?' She was very soft spoken and sympathetic.

I then asked, 'How big is the tumour? Is there a cure?'

Dr Afif looked at me, and with a very soft tone explained that the tumour was about the size of a pea, very small.

She then said, 'I will leave you two alone, and if you have any more questions then I am around.'

After she left the room, there was a deadly silence. It was the type of silence you feel before a terrible storm. In this case – a hurricane. We were unable to understand or analyse the information given. I was feeling an immense pain.

My voice was stuck in my throat, and the words could not come out of my mouth. My tears were frozen, and couldn't find a way out of my eyes. While I am writing this I am feeling exactly the same as I felt on the day.

I left the room and went to see Khushil. I thanked the nurse for looking after him. I sat with Khushil and started talking to him as normal. I asked him, 'How was your lunch?' He said to me, 'Mum, they make good pasta! I won't mind staying here if they gave me pasta again tomorrow.' He then said, 'Mum, you are a very good cook, but I would suggest that you learn how to make pasta from the chef here at the hospital.' As with anything, Khushil had a very particular taste. He always liked his food to be presented in a certain way. If he did not like the way the food was presented then he would not even taste it.

After about half an hour of talking to Khushil, my senses had somewhat recovered from the news. I told Khushil, 'I will be back in ten minutes' then found an empty room. As soon as I sat there, my heart sank. I started analysing the situation. I quickly found the doctor and asked her, 'Are you sure that what you told me is correct? How can you be sure that Khushil has definitely been diagnosed with cancer?' I was not doubting the ability or the intelligence of the doctors who had made the decision, it was more my ability to accept the facts and deal with the situation. Bhavesh and I were in the early stages of denial.

Dr Afif was very polite and told me that the reports were sent to the UCLH team because the hospital initially doubted the diagnosis too, but the UCLH team had confirmed it. She reaffirmed that we would soon be appointed a doctor, who would be looking after Khushil going forward.

Obviously, this was not what I wanted to hear. I went into a freeze mode and walked to the little waiting room. Now at this point, I couldn't stop tears coming out of my eyes. For Bhavesh and I, it felt like our world had ended. I couldn't believe that from having a perfect life and a perfect family, God had suddenly brought us to zero. God had decided to take away everything that He had given me. In a second, it felt like we had lost everything. There was nothing left to live for. Bhavesh requested the nurse to sit with Khushil, and then came to see me. We both came to our senses, we both cried. I just couldn't stop crying; I didn't know how to stop crying. My brain had lost its thinking power, and my heart had lost all the emotions. We felt as if happiness had been erased from our lives.

At that point, I rang my dad. He is someone I need the most when I am in pain, just as Khushil needed me. I told him, through tears, exactly what the doctor had told us. I felt even worse just saying it. Speaking it made it real. It felt as if my life had come to a standstill. After around an hour we went back to see Khushil. He asked me where I'd been, and I lied to him, saying 'We were with the doctor discussing your scan result.'

In the hour that Bhavesh and I spent together, we had decided that we would not tell Khushil about his diagnosis. We wanted to protect him, and let him live his life as normal. We wanted the best possible life for our son.

Life is unpredictable. Even if you know what is going to come, there are only two things which are certain. One of them is change. The other is death. No situation is permanent. Good things cannot last forever, but in the same way, bad cannot last too. There will always be a change, and you must react accordingly. How well you react is down to what you are made of.

I truly believe that happiness is a choice, and not just a result. It is only you who can make yourself happy. Even though there are times when it might seem as if God has forsaken you, believe in Him. Believe that God will only give you pain that you can bear, to understand your own strengths and weaknesses. Believe that God has already thought of the situation you are going through. He has already prepared the cushions to soften your fall. If He pushes you to the edge of the cliff, then he will either catch you or teach you how to cope with the situation.

For Bhavesh and I, God's cushion came in the form of the lovely people around us, who supported us, and helped us to get through this. I might have been strong, but there were so many forces that helped to keep me upright through the winds of change. No matter the situation, life goes on, and so must you. God will always be with you.

LIFE With DIPG
(Diffuse Intrinsic Pontine Glioma)

The 26th March 2015 was the first day of the toughest period of our lives. We were shifted to a special room. Bhavesh and I tried to stay calm, not letting Khushil realise how serious and painful the situation was. I could barely sleep. I was not ready to accept the diagnosis. I just kept thinking that a squint in the eye could not be a symptom of a tumour. Again, I was in denial. I didn't want to believe it. I hadn't spoken to a specialist doctor, I hadn't seen any medical reports. That was enough for me to believe that the diagnosis was a mistake. I was completely lost, and had lost the capacity to think. I didn't know what I was doing. If someone asked me to do something, then I would just do it, without realising what I was doing or what I had been told to do. Everything was numb.

Hayley rang me that day, as I hadn't texted or called her. She was very worried, and asked, 'Is everything ok? How is Khushil?' Again, I didn't think about what I was saying. I just told her straight out, 'Khushil has been diagnosed with a brain tumour, which is cancerous.' Hayley was shocked. I clearly remember all she said was, 'Nam, can I call you back?' After couple of hours she called me again, and said, 'Don't worry, Nam, I am with you and any help you need just call me. I will take care of your work side, you just concentrate on Khushil and keep me informed.' Her call gave me peace of mind that I didn't have to worry about work.

We were told that Khushil would have to be admitted at the hospital until he could be shifted to UCLH, as he needed special care. I had a phone call that day with someone from UCLH, who informed me that we would have an appointment with Dr Shankar on the 1st of April 2015. Dr Shankar would be Khushil's consultant, moving forward. Along with being an incredible doctor, Dr Shankar is an Honorary Senior Lecturer & Consultant in Paediatric & Adolescent Oncology.

At that point, we were not sure how long Khushil would be staying in hospital, but of course we were intending to stay with him the whole time – so I called Shantaba and Jalpaben to let them know.

Khushil was a very clever boy. He didn't ask me, but he clearly knew something was happening, so he spoke to the doctor and enquired as to what the problem was. The doctor explained to Khushil that he had a small tumour, which needed treatment. That afternoon, Khushil suddenly had problems with his vision. He was seeing everything double. He got very scared by this, and we were scared too. The doctor came and gave him some medication, and he felt better after a couple of hours. The next day, a team of doctors and researchers came around with the camera. Khushil and I were sitting playing cards. They called me outside of the room, and asked me whether I would mind if they filmed Khushil. I felt a little uncomfortable with this, and questioned them about why they wanted to do it.

The doctors told me, 'Because DIPG is very rare, there is not enough information about the symptoms, and hence we would like to use Khushil as an example to create awareness in opticians and GP.' They would be using the video of Khushil as a way of educating doctors, to help them detect the tumour at an early stage. They informed me that the video would be shown to opticians and GPs, to help them in future.

I went into the room and asked Khushil if he was happy to tell the entire process that he had gone through at the hospital to the doctors, as they wanted to use that to educate GP and opticians. He instantly replied, 'Yes, I am happy to do that. If it is going to help other kids, then why not?'

While he was happy to help with the video, Khushil was now getting a bit agitated, because he was missing school. I spoke to the doctor at the hospital and asked about whether it was okay for us to go home. They told us that we could take Khushil home, but if there were any problems then we must come back immediately. This was a huge relief, and we came back home late on Friday evening.

That weekend was really difficult. We didn't know what to do. This was the first time when we were alone, without any doctors or nurses around. It was just us, looking after Khushil. The time that we were alone made us realise the enormity of what had just happened. We'd gone from having the perfect family to feeling as if we'd lost everything. God gave us life, but took away our oxygen. I couldn't sleep. I kept looking at Khushil the whole night. I was scared of losing him. Every time I looked at him I felt more and more scared, as if every passing moment was carrying me closer to a future without my son.

While I was worried and feeling stressed, I still had hope. We would be meeting Dr Shankar on the 1st, and I hoped that he might have a different diagnosis of Khushil's tumour. He might tell me that it was a mistake, and that they had simply misdiagnosed. He might tell me that it was a normal tumour, which could be operated on, and that Khushil would be fine.

Finally, the big day arrived, and we had an appointment with Dr Shankar. The 1st of April is our wedding anniversary. It is safe to say that this was the worst one ever. Our friend Jalpaben accompanied us to the hospital. We were very nervous, and lots was going through my mind. I was still hoping that Dr Shankar would give us good news. We had an appointment for 9am. The time was going extremely slow. Every minute felt like a year.

Dr Shankar called us into his room, and we all followed him with the hope that he was going to give us some different news.

The first thing he did was to check Khushil. He then asked us when we'd first noticed the squint in his eye, before arranging an extra MRI scan. The scan was booked for the very next day. After asking a few questions about Khushil, Dr Shankar requested that Khushil be taken by a nurse for a few routine check-ups, whilst he had a discussion with Bhavesh and I.

Dr Shankar hesitated before he started talking to us. He then said, 'I have checked the scan results sent through to us by Northwick Park Hospital, and we've had a meeting here to discuss them. I'm sorry to confirm to you that Khushil does have DIPG.'

He then continued, explaining the symptoms and prognosis of the DIPG. He explained to us that this type of tumour is classified as Grade 4, because of the seriousness and the symptoms of it. Unfortunately, DIPG has no cure, and they have yet to see a patient survive this condition. The only treatment available was radiotherapy – which would reduce the size of the tumour and stagnate the growth for 3-6 months, before it started re-growing. The radiotherapy can only be done once, and cannot be repeated.

Dr Shankar finished by saying, 'The maximum life span of a person diagnosed with DIPG, is 6-9 months.'

At this point, we were stunned. All I could say was, 'Are you sure? How do you know without any tests? Can you check it again?'

I just didn't want to believe him. I wasn't ready to accept it. Somehow, I had lost my senses. I was completely unaware of my surroundings. I was blank, and had lost the ability to speak or hear or smell. All I could feel was immense pain. Even at this moment, three years on, writing about it makes me feel the same. I was trying to stay strong for Khushil, and somehow I did. Somehow, I made it back from the hospital. When we reached Kingsbury station, Bhavesh requested that Jalpaben take Khushil home with her, just for the time being. Khushil and Hem (Jalpaben's son) were good friends, and it was the Easter holidays. Hem was at home. So, Jalpaben said to Khushil, 'Come back to my house and play with Hem for a little while', which Khushil seemed happy to do.

Bhavesh and I went home. Still, I was completely unaware of what was going on, but when I walked through the door my brain started to process things. 9 months, that was all I had. It takes 9 months to give birth to a child, and from that moment onwards you are meant to have the baby, your baby, with you for the rest of your life. And now, the doctor had given me just 9 months before my baby, my son, would be taken away. I would be losing my only child, my Khushil, forever. I cried and cried, and Bhavesh cried with me. All we wanted was for someone to come and tell us that it was a mistake, and that Khushil would be fine. But it didn't happen. We spent an hour crying and cursing ourselves and fate, trying to analyse our lives, and thinking what we had done wrong to be so harshly punished by God.

I believe in God, and feel that He is there to protect us in one way or the other. As per my religion, we believe that just as God decides the day of our birth, he also decides the day on which we will die. Our fate is already written, before we are born. God has decided who our parents will be, how our life will turn out, and the manner of our death. Every moment is pre-planned by Him. The Bhagwat (Hindu Holy Book) teaches us that whatever God does is ultimately for our own good. I agree with this, but to this day I still cannot convince myself that taking Khushil away from us was good, in any way, shape or form.

After that hour of fighting with ourselves, and with God, we decided (again) that we would never let Khushil know about the prognosis. We also resolved not to tell other people about Khushil's tumour. We wanted him to live life as normally as possible. There were a few people we told, such as Shantaba, Jalpaben, our very few relatives, and our managers. When I told him, one of my managers, Richard, said, 'Nam, my wife tells me that our children are the gift of God, and we don't know how long the gift is going to last.'

Now, readers, you must be thinking what is this DIPG? Let me give you some information about it.

What is DIPG?

DIPG is a tumour located in the middle of the brain stem. The brain stem is the bottommost portion of the brain, connecting the cerebrum with the spinal cord. As per Wikipedia: The majority of brain stem tumours occur in the pons and are diffusely infiltrating (they grow amidst the nerves), and therefore cannot be surgically removed.

Symptoms of DIPG

- Problems with eye movement, difficulty looking to the side, double vision because of the loss of alignment of eyes, drooping eyelids and inability to close the eyes completely.

- Facial weakness.

- Hearing problems.

- Trouble chewing or swallowing (not only swallowing food and water even own saliva), gagging while eating.

75

- Limb weakness, difficulty standing or walking, abnormal gaits, unbalanced limbs movements. Headache.

- Nausea and vomiting from brain swelling or hydrocephalus. (hydrocephalus is a condition in which the flow of cerebrospinal fluid around the brain is blocked), causing an increase in pressure inside the skull.

DIPG Symptom Management and End of Life Care (dipgregistery.org)

The symptoms below increase from time of progression to the end of life, ultimately affecting the quality of life.

- Constipation.

- Headache (headache and seizures).

- Pain.

- Nausea/Vomiting.

- Anxiety.

- Sleeping disturbance/Fatigue.

- Communication Difficulties (verbal and non-verbal).

- Passing of urine.

- Secretions.

- Breathing problems.

- Decrease in food and fluid intake.

There is no known cause of DIPG, but it only occurs in

young children. There has been ongoing research into DIPG, but not enough, at the moment, to find a cure.

A child diagnosed with DIPG today faces the same prognosis as a child diagnosed 40 years ago. Unfortunately, there is no chance of survival.

Getting back to our second day, 2nd of April, we had an appointment at 11am. We met Dr Shankar again. Clearly, I still had hope in my eyes, as Dr Shankar immediately apologised to me again and informed me that he genuinely had nothing which could help, as what he had said the previous day was true. Dr Shankar has been a great support to us. He looked after us during those difficult days, and is such a soft hearted and genuine person. That day we also met a specialist, who said that they needed to give Khushil a blood test and a lumbar puncher. If we gave permission, then she wanted to get 2 samples of each. The appointment for that was booked for the 3rd April 2015. The reason they needed these was twofold. Firstly, one sample would go to the laboratory that UCLH used to get the reports for Khushil. The second sample would be sent to another laboratory, which they used for samples when researching about DIPG. I consulted with Bhavesh and Khushil. Khushil being Khushil, he was always concerned about the greater good, and was happy to give two lots of blood samples and two lots of lumbar puncher samples. He truly had the mind of a scientist, and was more than happy to take part in any research with the aim of increasing the longevity of other people's lives.

We spent nearly the whole day at UCLH having his test

done, but Khushil never once complained about the pain. Even during the lumbar punctures, which are very uncomfortable, he didn't say a word. He just stayed calm and behaved in a mature manner.

Although we had resolved not to tell Khushil, it was hard, because he was a clever boy. He used to ask me, 'What did the doctor say?' and I would just tell him the first thing that came to my mind. Bhavesh and I were a bit all over the place in terms of our behaviour and actions. Khushil almost certainly noticed this, but he was clever enough to make me believe that he believed me, for the most part. He used to ask us why we were acting worried, and then asked us why we had changed. He used to say to Bhavesh, 'You have changed, but Mum is the same.' He always told me, 'Mum, you are strong.' Even during this period, where he was suffering, Khushil was looking after me.

Eventually, the time arrived when Bhavesh and I had to face up to the problem, make the decision on what we were going to do, and decide how we were going to cope with the situation. Our main aim was not to make things any worse. We had been given nine months. In our minds, we had already wasted ten or more days of that nine months, so we had approximately eight months and twenty days left. We had to decide whether these would be distressing, or whether we would make the most of the time we had left. It wasn't really a choice. With this in mind, Bhavesh and I made a list of all the things that Khushil wanted to do, and started planning how we could make sure they happened.

Still, even while we wrote the list, I was not ready to

accept what Dr Shankar had told us. Looking at Khushil, one would never suspect that he had any problems. He always had a smile on his face, and radiated happiness. Whenever somebody asked, 'How are you Khushil?' he would always answer the same – 'I am fine.' No situation could change this answer, as you will see in later chapters.

For a child to stay happy, even knowing that he has a brain tumour, is a big thing. Really, it's quite incredible. Obviously, we never told him the seriousness of the disease, but we thought he didn't need to know that. As parents, we wanted to protect him, and I am sure that all you readers can understand that. More than anything, we didn't want him to lose hope. We wanted him to believe in his heart of hearts that he would get better, and that he would grow up to become a scientist or a zoologist. We didn't want him to stop living his best life possible.

Deciding to try and be positive, even for Khushil, was an incredibly hard decision to make. It meant taking all the stress and pain that Bhavesh and I felt, and putting it one side. However, looking at Khushil and his lovely smiling face gave us strength. Not just his smile, but his determination to always shine in any situation, and always achieve what he set out to do. If Khushil could do that, then we could do this for him.

While we were making decisions on what to do, Khushil started suffering the side effects of steroids. He had a swollen, puffy face. His appetite had increased, and due to water retention and swelling he looked much bigger. He was getting tired and feeling weaker. Incredibly,

79

despite all of this, he didn't stop going to school. He even made sure that as soon as he was off the steroids, within two months he looked exactly the same as before.

We had an appointment with Dr Chan on the 8th April 2015 regarding Khushil's radiotherapy treatment. Dr Chan was Khushil's radiotherapy specialist; she explained how the whole process would work. It was a six week treatment, which would start from the 13th April 2015, and the treatment would be given Monday to Friday every week.

Dr Chan told me that the radiotherapy treatment was a one-time thing, and could not be repeated. Then she explained to me about the side effects of the radiotherapy. This includes headaches, weakness in limbs, hair loss, brain swelling, skin irritation, feeling sick, dizzy, and much more. After the appointment with Dr Chan, we met the specialist, to make the mask for Khushil's face. The face mask is made to measure on the day. A special type of material is warmed up, then put on the face, so that it moulds and takes the shape and size of the face. You can either leave the mask plain or have some pictures. Khushil's mask had pictures of dragons on, as he believed that dragons are very strong.

Khushil was admitted to UCLH for the first week of his radiotherapy treatment, on the week commencing 13th April 2015. I called my mum for help from India. She had come to our rescue at a very crucial stage. At the same time, Neelaben (Bhavesh's sister) had come as well. It was a very big decision for her, as she had come alone. She had left her 8-year-old son, Kush, with his dad and this was the first time she had done so. While Khushil was admitted, he made me get his schoolwork from his teachers, so that he did not miss his studies.

After his treatment in the morning, we would spend the whole day playing with Khushil. We'd spend time on the PlayStation, Xbox, and even playing table tennis. Khushil was an excellent table tennis player. Initially, UCLH did not have the facilities for this, but they were kind enough to make the arrangements and set up a table just for him. Their dedication was incredible, and we all appreciated this so much. They also arranged special things in the afternoon, like painting or movie time to keep the kids happy while they were in the hospital. All the kids were very well looked after.

We were allowed to take Khushil out as well, so we decided to treat him by taking him to Pizza Hut. He loved it, and he also really enjoyed the walk to the restaurant. Even though the hospital staff were fantastic, Khushil didn't enjoy spending so much time in the hospital, and it felt good for him to get outdoors.

Dr Shankar would often visit Khushil while he was admitted in UCLH. One day Bhavesh had gone downstairs to the shop to get something for Khushil, and I had gone out of his room to get him a game. At that time, Dr Shankar came to visit. Khushil took the opportunity to ask him, 'Dr Shankar, are you a cancer doctor?' Dr Shankar was surprised. When the nurse told us about this, we asked Khushil about how he knew the doctor's full name. He said, 'I saw it on the first day, from the name badge he was wearing.' This was not really a surprise, as we should never have underestimated

Khushil's intelligence. He had obviously done his research, and knew what he was talking about. He also asked us questions, such as, 'Why do we come to the MacMillan Cancer Centre for my treatment?' It was not that he did not know, more that he kept asking us in order to check whether we were telling him the truth.

Khushil had to get his blood test done every other week during his treatment. One day we went for his blood test, but due to his radiotherapy treatment and getting his blood taken so many times, no blood came out. The doctor at UCLH told me that Khushil's veins had dried, and hence it was taking longer. The doctors tried a few times, and also tried punchering him, but still no blood came out. By that time it was almost 1600, and we had been in the UCLH since 9am.

I was getting agitated, as we'd seen about four different doctors, and they'd all tried roughly the same thing – with no results. Even after all this, Khushil never once complained. He stayed extremely strong, and this gave me strength. I then told the doctors that, if they would allow me to, I wanted to take Khushil home. I would not let them touch him with anymore needles that day. They allowed us to leave.

As I mentioned, radiotherapy treatment comes with a great number of side effects. To all of the specialists' surprise, Khushil tolerated the treatment extremely well, and had no signs of side effects. The doctors said that they had never seen any child so strong. With this in mind, we were discharged on Friday the 17th April 2015.

For the next week, Khushil selected between 8am to

8.10am as his treatment time, so that he could attend school. We used to drive to Kingsbury station every morning, park the car, then use the underground to get to Euston. It usually took us 45 minutes to reach the UCLH, with Khushil carrying his school bag and wearing his school uniform. It took 10 minutes for his treatment every morning, and then we would get back to Kingsbury Station, and from there we would go to drop Khushil at school. He did not miss a single day of school because of his treatment. Throughout his six weeks of radiotherapy treatment, Khushil did not complain about anything. Even when his face swelled up, meaning his mask didn't fit him anymore, he did not say a bad word. He would always say, 'I am fine. It's okay, it doesn't take long to complete the treatment, don't worry.' This made Bhavesh and I stronger too. Even if we knew he was suffering, he made us believe that it was easier for him than it was.

Laura (Khushil's play specialist) was very helpful, and looked after Khushil every single day when he went for his radiotherapy. She made sure that he was not worried or stressed whilst going through his treatment. Laura took care of every little thing, like wishing Khushil good morning, telling him he looked smart in his school uniform, and also talking to him about his day at school. She asked him what he would like to watch while he had radiotherapy, and made sure that she had the CDs to show him. Khushil had requested SpongeBob and Dynamo magic CDs – and as requested Laura had them ready. She had the whole series of Dynamo's "Impossible Magics" for Khushil to watch whilst he was waiting for his treatment. The treatment finished on

22nd May 2015. Let me tell you all something surprising – Khushil is an example of the success that comes to those who refuse to give up. During his treatment, Khushil received an award for "Star Patient during Radiotherapy", which they gave to him as a laminated certificate, with Dynamo's picture on it. The team also gifted him a watch and vouchers on the last day of his treatment. This was very touching, and to this day Bhavesh and I are extremely grateful for their help and support. The team was very friendly, and even a year later when we visited again, they still all remembered Khushil. On the first day of the treatment every single team member who passed by called Khushil by name and remembered him. They said, 'How could we forget Khushil? His smile is unforgettable.'

The radiotherapy treatment would take up to 6 weeks to have any impact, so we had an MRI scan to check whether the treatment had been successful or not. The scan took place on the 7th July 2015. It had worked. We were so relieved by this, that for a moment it felt as if Khushil had been cured. Following this, we had regular appointments with Dr Shankar, twice a month, and a home visit from a UCLH nurse once a month. Khushil, as usual, kept on going to school and had the quality of life that he deserved. I had stopped working since the day Khushil was diagnosed with the tumour, so that I could be there if he needed me. By that point, it had been nearly a year.

Now, Khushil decided it was time for me to get back to work. He said that he wanted me to start working again whilst he was at school. I had a meeting with

Hayley, and asked her whether it would be okay for me to return. I was still a bit worried and scared, but it was more motherly instinct that was making me feel that way. Bhavesh kept on saying to me, 'All you need is to start working. It's nothing else. You are worrying unnecessarily.'

Bhavesh never liked talking about Khushil's tumour, and still doesn't. He never opened up, and I must say that sometimes it was frustrating. I couldn't share my worry with anyone, and was concerned that Bhavesh was not sharing his feelings. I could never tell how he actually felt. However, I kept trying and trying, and eventually got through to him. We had a long talk about how he felt, and from that moment onwards I felt at ease, knowing that he wasn't just keeping it all in. This helped me to cope with the situation, somewhat.

Shortly after I'd spoken with Hayley, Khushil had another scan. The time between the scans and the doctor's appointments always went extremely slow. On the day when we were due to receive the results, Bhavesh had decided not to come, as he had a superstition that if he came then the scan results would be negative. This didn't bother me, and so I went by myself. I still had that horrible feeling in my stomach, that worry, but my heart wanted to prove that my worry was unnecessary.

Khushil in Italy, August 2015

Every time we went to see Dr Shankar, he would come and get us from the waiting room. He always made sure that we felt assured, safe and comfortable, and that he was always happy to help. That day, when Dr Shankar came out to get me, the first question he asked was, 'Where's Dad?' I told him the truth about why Bhavesh didn't want to come. My heart was beating very fast at that moment, and my face must have been showing my stress and worry. Dr Shankar took me into his office, and asked me a few routine questions. Then he opened up his computer and got up the scan results.

'Mum, I'm afraid I don't have good news for you. The tumour has started re-growing.'

He then showed me the comparison between the last and the current images of scan. Normally the radiotherapy kills the cancer growth for at least 6 months or more. However, it had been 1 year since the treatment. I was speechless. Again, I had a brain freeze. I lost the ability to analyse information. I heard what Dr Shankar was saying, but my brain wouldn't allow me to understand it.

The staff were very worried for me, and said that they couldn't let me go home on my own. Dr Shankar said, 'I will call your husband to pick you up.' I assured him that I was fine to return home on my own. One of the nurses offered, but again I refused. They gave me a number, and made me promise to call or text the number as soon as I arrived back. Before leaving, I made a request to Dr Shankar. I wanted him to see whether it was at all possible for Khushil to have a small dose of radiotherapy treatment again. He told me that he would try his best, but couldn't promise anything.

Khushil was still at school when I arrived home. Bhavesh and I didn't speak to each other for a whole hour. We didn't know what to say. Later in the afternoon I had my appointment with Hayley. I told her that the tumour had started growing again, but that I still wanted to come back to work, as this was Khushil's wish. Hayley agreed to this, and we arranged for me to start working again during the following week. After the meeting, I picked up Khushil from school. The first question he asked was, 'How was the meeting, what did the doctor say?' I told him that the scan result was good, and then he started teasing me, saying, 'Look, you were worrying for no reason!'

Dr Shankar rang me the following week, and informed me that they were willing to consider another dose of radiotherapy. However, he reaffirmed that this was not common, and that the risks were extremely high. At that stage, Bhavesh and I were willing to try anything. Even the tiniest chance of success was enough for us. After another meeting with Dr Shankar, it was agreed that Khushil would receive a short 2-week radiotherapy treatment. Due to the risks involved, it would take more time to plan for this treatment.

Khushil was always very conscious about how he looked. The steroids had an impact on his appearance, making him looked blotted and changing the shape of his face – which he was very unhappy about. Dr Shankar started him off on a low dose of steroids, for a short period of time. The treatment started on the 4th July 2016 and ended on the 16th July 2016. Khushil made the decision that he would have the treatment every day after school, at 16:00. He stayed very strong throughout the whole thing. Just like the first time, he tolerated the treatment well, and didn't show any side effects. The radiotherapy team were amazed by Khushil's tolerance, as were Bhavesh and I. I don't know where he found the strength to attend a whole day of school and then go for radiotherapy treatment, but that was Khushil. He never let his smile and positive attitude fade.

On the 1st September 2016, Khushil had a scan, which would tell us whether the treatment had worked or not. We had a meeting on the 7th September 2016, to discuss the results with Dr Shankar. This time I wasn't going to take any risks, so Bhavesh came with me.

Dr Shankar sat us down and sympathetically informed us that unfortunately the treatment had not worked. There was a negligible difference in the size of the tumour. Khushil did not have much time left. I asked, 'How much time, do you think?' and Dr Shankar informed me that while he couldn't give a specific time limit, we had 'roughly speaking, 3-4 months.'

As you'll have noticed, readers, 3-4 months represented a significant decrease in time. And I was still not ready to accept the diagnosis. Khushil's attitude, positivity, and quality of life had not changed one bit compared to how it was pre-diagnosis. My heart always said that there would be a day when we'd go for an appointment, and Dr Shankar would say, 'Sorry, it was a mistake and Khushil is fine.' I promise, I would have walked out without saying anything and invited the whole team at UCLH for a celebratory dinner, forgetting the stress and anguish that we had gone through for over a year and half.

Although this did not happen, I appreciate the honesty of Dr Shankar and his team. I have always had fantastic experiences with the NHS. Their service was not just 'for the sake of doing it'. Khushil was more than just 'a patient', and they treated him with care and respected all his wishes. Not only did they look after Khushil, but they treated me and Bhavesh with the utmost affection and understanding. This didn't just apply to UCLH, but Northwick Park Hospital too, Tanya, Catherine, speech therapists and dieticians, plus our GP – Dr Sayed. We had no issue in getting appointments to see doctors and consultants. The nurses were ready to help any time, day or night. All of these dedicated medical professionals still look after us, call us, and visit us to make sure that we are okay. I can't thank them enough for their support.

Khushil's Special Bond with Claremont High School

गुरुर्ब्रह्मा गुरुर्वष्णिु र्गुरुर्देवो महेश्वरः

गुरु साक्षात परब्रह्मा तस्मै श्रीगुरवे नमः

"GururBrahma GururVishnu Gururdevo Maheswarah

Guruh Saakshaat ParaBrahma Tasmai Sri Gurve Namah"

And the English translation of this goes like this:

"The Teacher is the Lord Brahma because he creates the knowledge inside us. The Teacher is the Lord Vishnu because he preserves and operates the knowledge in our mind on to the right path. The Teacher is the Lord Mahesh or Shiva because he destroys the wrong thoughts and transforms us with the right kind of knowledge. Thus, The Teacher or The Guru is the live supreme God and we salute and bow to our teacher."

आचार्य देवो भव पर संस्कृत नबिंध

"Acharya Devo Bhava"

Indian tradition equates the teacher to god, as the Sanskrit hymn goes "Acharya devo bhava".

Dear readers, the reason I have started with the Sanskrit Shlokas is because these Shlokas define Claremont High School's ethics, and its teachers.

Today, it's believed that the world has changed, and

the teachings of our holy book aren't as prominent anymore. But I would like to say, today, that the world hasn't changed. There are schools, teachers and people in the world who define the Sanskrit Shlokas, and hold themselves to a higher standard.

Khushil had a very unique and a special bond with the teachers at Claremont High School. The school supported us through every stage of his tumour. They made the necessary arrangements and changes to fit Khushil's requirements, including making arrangements for his school work to be delivered to our home while he was in hospital.

I can still picture the day when I went to the school with the first letter that Dr Shankar gave us, providing an overview of the illness and prognosis. I met with Mr Gareth Riggs (Head of Year 8 & 9). When I showed him the letter, he was absolutely shocked. All he could say was that he was so sorry to hear about the diagnosis, and that the school would do everything within their power to help Khushil.

As I've already mentioned, Khushil loved going to school. For this reason, he absolutely wouldn't agree to hospital appointments during school time. Consultant appointments generally happened after school, because Khushil wouldn't want to miss even his first lesson. A classic example of how much Khushil enjoyed going to school – most parents generally wake their children up in the mornings to get them ready. In our case, Khushil used to set an alarm for us, then wake us so that he wasn't late! He would set four alarms in total. One for Bhavesh, one for me, and two for himself.

Each and every teacher at Claremont was fantastic, but there were a few teachers who were very close to Khushil. These were Mr Riggs (Head of year 8 & 9), Ms Taylor (Deputy Head of year 9), Ms Patel (Geography Teacher), Ms Perkins (English Teacher), Ms Arbani (Science Teacher), Ms Chikvaidze (Maths Teacher), Ms Carswell (Duke of Edinburgh Manager), Mr Page (Senior Co-ordinator)), Ms Shah (Year 11) and Ms McGuiness (Class Teacher).

There were only a few teachers who knew that Khushil had been diagnosed with a brain tumour, and only Mr Riggs, Ms Taylor, Ms Thomas and couple of other teachers knew that it was DIPG. We had requested that the school told as few teachers as possible about it, as we wanted Khushil to live his life to the full, on his own terms.

Mr Riggs

Every single relationship that Khushil had in Claremont School was special. However, the one relationship that Khushil cherished the most was with Mr Riggs.

Khushil loved the phrase, 'Never judge a book by its cover.' The reason I say this is because if you don't know Mr Riggs, he gives the impression of being quite strict. He always wants his students to be wearing the correct school uniform, with polished shoes. He has an eagle eye; no student can escape from Mr Riggs if they are misbehaving, or if they aren't dressed properly. But once you know him, he has a diamond heart. I use the word diamond, because diamonds are precious and rare. Mr Riggs may appear hard from the outside, but he has a sparkly shine inside.

Mr Riggs loved Khushil, not just because Khushil was suffering from DIPG, but because Mr Riggs admired Khushil's care for education. Mr Riggs looked after Khushil from day one, but in a way that gave him space. He didn't make it obvious, but he was keeping an eye on Khushil all the time. During break times he would pass casually by Khushil, without making it known that he was there. Furthermore, Mr Riggs was extremely good to us. He never made us feel as if he was too busy to talk, and would always take time out of his busy schedule to update us. This was even more impressive given that he was the head of year, which meant that Khushil wasn't the only student whom he had to look after. Even after 18:00, when all of the students had gone home, he would call me just to check that we were okay and coping well. This was incredibly thoughtful of him, and shows just how kind-hearted he is.

Throughout this book, you will read many examples which illustrate the special relationship between Khushil and Mr Riggs. One such example was when Khushil's year group were going to Thorpe Park, whilst the year 8 group were going to the zoo. Knowing that Khushil loved going to the zoo, Mr Riggs took him along on the year 8 trip. Khushil loved this, and when he came back we discussed with him and Mr Riggs about the day. Mr Riggs said that he enjoyed spending time with Khushil, and that there was one particular section, in the reptile area, where they spent 45 minutes (as it was feeding time). Bhavesh and I were touched that Mr Riggs had the patience to stand in one place for 45 minutes, just because Khushil wanted to. Then Mr Riggs said to us, 'I recently watched Sir David Attenborough's interview, where he spent 30 minutes in the same place where Khushil spent 45. Genius minds think alike!' Both Bhavesh and I were extremely proud in that moment.

Khushil at London Zoo, July 2017 (Photo taken by Mr Riggs)

Mr Riggs puts the Shlokas that I mentioned in the beginning of the chapter into perspective. He is a teacher in the truest sense of the word, who proves that "Acharaya Devo Bhava". You will get to know a bit more know about Mr Riggs and how he supported us, later in this book. Mr Riggs is more like family to us now, than a teacher.

Ms Carswell

Ms Carswell is another person whom I absolutely must speak about. She has been an absolute angel, and went out of her way to help Khushil achieve his dream of achieving the Duke of Edinburgh Bronze Award (DofE). She did everything in her power to make this possible. Not only did she made special arrangements within the school, but she also made special arrangements in conjunction with the DofE team. She undertook special research on different places, to where she could take Khushil for his practice and his main expedition. Ms Carswell worked extremely hard, not just to make things possible for Khushil, but for other students too. Her readiness to help students at any cost and time is phenomenal.

Again, I am repeating myself, but Ms Carswell is also part of my family.

Mr Page

Mr Page entered Khushil's life a bit later in his journey, but when he did arrive, it was at the most crucial time.

Mr Page made it possible for Khushil to attend school every day, without any problems. He made sure that Khushil had a support teacher with him at all times, so that he could move around at school. When Mr Page was introduced to Khushil, Khushil was in a wheelchair and was unable to walk. Gradually, Khushil's difficulties increased, and he deteriorated. At every stage Mr Page made Khushil feel comfortable, and made it seem as if everything was possible, especially when it came to helping Khushil attend lessons.

The help from Claremont made it possible for Khushil to attend school every single day, without any problems. My heart was never worried when I dropped Khushil off, as I knew that he was in a safe place, and being looked after.

Just to give you an example, Mr Page would personally look after Khushil during lunch time, and made sure that Khushil had eaten enough. As Khushil's illness progressed, he had difficulties in swallowing. Even little things like making sure that Khushil had drunk enough water were important. Mr Page did everything possible, selflessly, with love and care.

It wasn't only the teachers who were supportive, but the students too. As I've explained, Khushil's appearance changed while he was on steroids. Despite this, there wasn't a single student who mocked him, or even asked him why he looked different. Every person at Claremont treated my son with the respect he deserved, and Bhavesh and I are so grateful for that.

Life Experiences

Khushil's attitude towards life, and his way of accepting whatever life threw at him, helped me and Bhavesh get through the most difficult period that we have ever experienced.

As I have previously mentioned, Bhavesh and I decided that we would protect Khushil, and not tell him about the terminal diagnosis. As per our decision, we decided to stay strong and started making a wish list.

Our list started with the help of Laura, from the UCLH team. During the radiotherapy treatment, Laura showed me a 'last wish form', which is essentially something that people can fill in before they pass on – with the aim being that UCLH and any relatives/friends can help them accomplish these goals. Filling in the form was incredibly emotional.

I wanted the best life for my son. Never had I imagined that I would ever have to complete this kind of form, especially not for my child. It was heartbreaking. Laura helped me to complete the form. You were allowed to write three wishes in total, labelled one to three in terms of priority. Khushil filled in all of the wishes the same – *I want to meet Dynamo*.

After submitting the wish form, Rays of Sunshine (who make the wishes happen) contacted us to say that they had only recently arranged a meeting for another child to meet Dynamo, and therefore Khushil would have to wait a while before it could be sorted. I replied back, asking them to do everything they could to help Khushil's wish come true. Within two weeks, Laura came to me and said, 'I have a date for Khushil to meet Dynamo – 11th May 2015!' Khushil was ecstatic about this, and he told all of his close friends about how excited he was to meet his idol. He was so looking forward to the meeting.

When the day came around, we met Dynamo alongside another family. This meant that Khushil had plenty of time to talk to Dynamo and get his autograph, and he showed us lots of his magic. I wouldn't want to lower what he did by calling them 'tricks', as they were not just tricks – it was real magic, and it was absolutely fascinating. Meeting Dynamo was an incredible experience. Rays of Sunshine had arranged for a limousine to pick us up from home and take us to the meeting. We then had lunch at Planet Hollywood, in Hays Market in Piccadilly. It was all very posh, and all thanks to Khushil.

When Dynamo first met Khushil, he said, 'What do you want me to do for you?'

Khushil brought out an old photo of himself and said, 'Do you see my picture here? I want to meet you when I look like this again.'

Dynamo replied, 'Sure, I will meet you again, I promise.'

Khushil said, 'I've got tickets for your show in October, can we meet then?', to which Dynamo said, 'Absolutely.'

We also brought along some pictures from our wall, for Dynamo to sign, plus Khushil took a picture of Laura – who is a big fan of Dynamo, and asked him to sign that too. Dynamo was incredibly sweet. He signed every single photo, and was so genuine, kind hearted, and down to earth.

Khushil with Dynamo, May 2015 (During Khushil's radiotherapy treatment)

After the meeting, we went for lunch in Planet Hollywood. There were big screens in the restaurant, with words written across them in big letters, saying, "Planet Hollywood Welcomes Khushil Pandya and his Family.........Have a great day!" This was truly amazing. It made Khushil feel so happy, and the smile on his face was enough to help Bhavesh and I forget the sorrow and pain, for a while anyway. As a final touch, we were sent a CD, containing all of the photos taken on the day.

Khushil loved animals, but he was especially fond of dogs. With this in mind, Laura secretly made arrangements for a special dog, named Cassie, to visit the UCLH and meet Khushil. This was the first time they had arranged this kind of surprise. They had given special vaccinations to the dog so that it could be brought to the radiotherapy treatment section. The picture of Khushil and Cassie was then put in the UCLH newsletter, in June 2015. Khushil was delighted with this, and Bhavesh and I were very happy too.

After the completion of Khushil's treatment on the 30th May 2015, the first place we visited was Woburn Safari. It was an amazing experience, where Khushil got to meet lots of different animals. Following that, we visited Longleat Safari, in July.

Khushil with Bhavesh and Namrata, Woburn Safari 2015, pretending that he is giving us blessings.

At that time, we had to plan our weekends, as they were always so busy. We wanted to make the absolute best of the time we had left. We'd go to the cinema, out to dinner, or if we had nothing planned then we'd make sure we went to Khushil's favourite places – WH Smith or Waterstones. Khushil also loved going to Lakeside shopping centre, as he loved Taco Bell. As I've mentioned, Khushil was incredibly precise and particular in his choices. He would decide where he got his hair cut, which restaurants we ate at, what brands he wore...every little thing that he did was decided by him, and nobody else. He was his own person, strong and comfortable in the knowledge of who he was.

Come August, Khushil wanted to go to Italy. He was fascinated by the history of cities like Rome. He wanted to visit Milan – the fashion capital, plus Capri and Venice. So, off we went! Khushil absolutely loved this holiday, and we were so happy that he was still able to enjoy it. He'd just finished his first radiotherapy treatment, and still had burns on both sides of his head behind his ears, along with missing hair, due to the treatment. The weather was absolutely scorching, so we were worried this would hurt him. Khushil being Khushil, he did not even mention this once, he just made the most of the holiday and had the best time possible.

Khushil with Bhavesh in Italy, 2016

On the 16th September, my sister Chaitali visited us for 10 days with her beautiful daughters, Mahi and Krupa, and her husband Parag. This was the first time that Khushil had stayed with his cousins, and he absolutely loved it. They loved him too. If you ask Mahi and Krupa about who they love the most, they will reply, 'Khushil bhaiyo' (bhaiyo meaning brother). Krupa is the youngest of the two. She said to me, 'I have only one request – that I get to hug Khushil every day.'

Now, if you remember, earlier on in this chapter I mentioned that Khushil asked Dynamo where he could meet him again, and that we had tickets for Dynamo's next show. On the day of the show, I received a call from Dynamo's PA. She said to me, 'Is this Khushil's mum? I am Dynamo's PA, and he remembers that he had promised to meet Khushil at the show tonight.' I just couldn't believe it. I was over the moon, and was so happy and excited for Khushil to be meeting his idol once again. The PA asked me not to tell Khushil, as they wanted it to be a surprise. She said she'd ring me after the show, and then we'd take Khushil backstage to meet Dynamo.

The show was incredible. Dynamo truly is the Magician Impossible, and the magic was absolutely jaw dropping. After the show, as planned, I got a call from the PA asking me to come towards the gate. When she came out, Khushil was confused and surprised. I just shook my head, pretending that I didn't know anything. We followed her backstage, and into an office. As soon as we got into the room, Dynamo came in behind us. Khushil couldn't believe it. He was speechless! He got very emotional and said, 'It's great that you remembered, Dynamo.' Dynamo told Khushil, 'You do look different compared to when I met you in May. You look very smart!' That made Khushil's day. Really, we couldn't have asked for anything more. It was just perfect.

Khushil with Dynamo (The Magician Impossible), October 2015

Bhavesh and I were determined to keep Khushil smiling. So, we decided to contact another idol of his – Steve Backshall.

Steve Backshall is the BBC TV presenter of "Deadly 60" and numerous other series, he's an all-round amazing individual. Steve was happy to meet Khushil before his show, and also sent us tickets. We met him on the 31st October 2015. Steve spoke to Khushil, and gave him an autograph. After the show Steve was giving autographs to everyone who attended, but the team generously let us spend some time backstage and gave Khushil another chance to speak with Steve. Again, it was a perfect example of the goodness of humanity, and Khushil had such a lovely time.

Khushil with his Idol Steve Backshall, October 2015

On the 7th November, Richard and Hayley had arranged for Khushil to watch Manchester United, his favourite football team, from the Old Trafford directors' box. On top of that, as if watching Man Utd play wasn't exciting enough, they'd also made sure that Khushil got to meet with two Man Utd legends – Sir Bobby Charlton and Sir Alex Ferguson. You can only imagine how happy Khushil was with this!

Khushil with Sir Alex Ferguson, November 2015

Before the start of the match, Sir Alex Ferguson asked Khushil, 'What will the score be?' and Khushil replied, '2-0.' Of course, it finished 2-0. Sir Bobby Charlton then took Khushil with him to a special room, which had the names of the best players in Man Utd history on the wall. Sir Bobby had a chat with Khushil, showing him the trophies and talking to him about his school. Both Sir Alex Ferguson and Sir Bobby Charlton were so kind and hospitable to Khushil, and I cannot thank them enough for this. They made Khushil feel incredibly special. Lee Martin also came down to meet Khushil, showed him his medal, and gave Khushil an autographed picture. After all that was finished, Khushil said to Sir Alex, 'Will the manager come up here?' to which Sir Alex said, 'Would you like to meet him?' Of course, Khushil said yes. Sir Alex then sent a message down, asking Louis Van Gaal to come up for a few minutes. I think it's in the culture of Man Utd that if they are making someone's wish come true, they make it the most memorable day of that person's life. Louis Van Gaal came up especially to meet with Khushil, gave him his autograph, and took some pictures.

This was not planned, but they made it possible just for Khushil. Every time something like this happened, it reminded me that no matter how hard life got, there would always be someone up there looking after us. This time God had sent Richard, Hayley and Michael to fulfil Khushil's wishes.

Khushil with Sir Bobby Charlton, November 2015

Khushil loved watching tennis, and supported Novak Djokovic. November is the time for the ATP Tour in London. Being optimistic, we got tickets for the final, hoping that Novak Djokovic and Roger Federer would be in the final. Bhavesh supports Roger Federer, and Khushil and I support Novak Djokovic. The 22nd November 2015 was the final in the O2 – this was the first time we were going to view a live Tennis match. The final was certainly worth a watch, as we were seeing two legends compete. Djokovic won, and history was made. As I previously mentioned, God can't be present at all places at once, so He sends his angels to help out. This time, He sent someone who took Khushil with him to get Novak's autograph.

This lovely man came from out of nowhere, and there was a queue of people waiting to go down, but he picked Khushil out from the queue and said, 'Let's go, I will take you down.' It wasn't that far, and I could clearly see Khushil, so I let him go. Then, something strange happened. The man came back and said, 'Security won't let two people go down on one ticket, so I gave mine to your son. Please keep an eye on him.' I couldn't believe it, I just thanked him from the bottom of my heart. He said, 'That's fine, I will get another chance.' And then he was gone.

God always looks after his children. Believe in Him, and He will help you, but you must be able to help yourself before God can truly assist. Khushil was extremely lucky that day. He got his autograph, and then Novak returned to him again and gave him another autograph. We searched for the man who had given us the ticket, but he was nowhere to be seen. What can you say? Angels really were looking out for us that day. Everyone goes through tough times in life, but at the same time God gives you good periods too. The day ended with another high note from Almighty.

Now, onto our next project – Khushil's birthday. Khushil was born on the 8th December. He would be thirteen that year. Bhavesh and I had planned to have a big birthday party, as he was going to be a teenager, so we wanted it to be extra special. Unfortunately, it wasn't easy, as the doctors suspected that the tumour would start re-growing by that time, and that the party might be a struggle if so. However, we tried to be optimistic. We didn't stop our planning, and booked a venue called Blue Ginger. Bhavikbhai and Helly had decided to come down from the USA, to give Khushil a surprise for his birthday. They had also planned to give Khushil a Segway for his birthday. We were really excited, and determined to make this a success.

The day started really good. Bhavikbhai and Helly had arrived, and the party went as planned. We were beating the odds. Khushil's health was good, and he was extremely happy with the gifts. I can remember Khushil's face opening all his gifts, and his sheer surprise that we had got him every single gift that he wanted. It was the most amazing moment of our life, to see him so happy. He said to me, 'Mum, how come I have got everything I thought of? I'm very happy, thank you! You are the best parents. I cannot ask for anything more.' To make it extra special, Bhavesh and I had created a picture book, where we requested that all of the guests wrote a message for Khushil. The messages written were so heart-warming and lovely. I was absolutely touched by this, and shed a few tears. The tears were a mixture of happiness, seeing Khushil so delighted and loved by everyone there, and sadness, knowing that we wouldn't be able to experience something like this again. Although I have tried to be brave, I cry sometimes when I am on my own – but that's okay.

Khushil's birthday celebration, 8th December 2015

Khushil was brilliant at table tennis. Despite the diagnosis, he was extremely focused, and would go with Bhavesh to play table tennis nearly every week at the leisure centre. Once, I went with them, and a trainer came up to me and said, 'If you would allow for it, I would love the chance to train your son. In a few months he'll be able to play locally, and then surely nationally.

112

If he's playing this good without any training, then with proper guidance and training he'll be unbeatable!' He then invited us to come along to his classes.

We went along for our first session, and the trainer told his students, 'Play against the new boy.' Khushil beat them all. The trainer turned to me and said, 'This is what I'm talking about, he is a gem!' Obviously, this was exciting, but knowing Khushil I didn't want to put pressure on him. I knew that if he really got into it then he wouldn't be able to stop playing, and he would achieve things regardless. Khushil was still keen on playing, but he wasn't interested in entering any competitions. Bhavesh and Khushil being best friends, they loved playing each other and competing – even when it came to football. Bhavesh supports Chelsea, and Khushil supported Man Utd. So, we were used to internal rivalry, and it made things fun!

On the 24th December 2015, my mother-in-law passed away. We all went to India, as a family, to deal with the loss. I miss her greatly, as we had a fantastic relationship. She was like a second mother to me, and looked after me when I needed her.

Khushil at Heathrow airport, travelling to India, 2015

While we were in India, Bhavesh's maternal uncle Dilipmama had arranged for Khushil to watch a live concert of his favourite Indian singer, Arijit Singh. He got Khushil front row tickets! In a pure coincidence, Arijit sang all the songs that Khushil loved the most. It was a lovely night, and a really memorable experience. My father-in-law's friend also arranged for Khushil to meet his favourite contestant from Indian Idol Junior – Nirvesh Dave. Nirvesh was absolutely lovely, and so humble. He met with Khushil on 10th January 2016, gave him his autograph, and spent lots of time just talking with him.

With all this going on, there was no time to stop! March 8th 2016 was another big day. I had to get special permission from Claremont for Khushil to take the day off school, and it was even harder to get permission from Khushil himself! But, luckily, everyone agreed. The reason being that Manchester United had arranged a special day, where Khushil would meet the team, and then we would watch them train. This was so incredible that even Khushil couldn't say no to missing school.

We had a really early start that day, leaving at 6am. This time it was just me and Khushil. When we got there, Khushil was on top of the world. He loved watching the team train, and then every single team player came up to meet the kids. They all had a chat, took lots of photographs and gave their autographs to Khushil. All the players made Khushil feel really special. However, I should mention one particular incident that stood out. Khushil's favourite player was Wayne Rooney, who at that time had just come back from holiday. So, he wasn't in training that day. When Louis Van Gaal came, he asked, 'What is your name? How are you? Where do you come from?' Then he sat Khushil on his lap, and asked him, 'Did you meet all the players? Are you happy?' Khushil said, 'Yes, I met the players, but I want to meet Rooney as well. Is he not going to come? I like the whole team but Rooney is my favourite.' Louis Van Gaal said, 'Well, let's see what I can do!'

Khushil with Louis Van Gaal (Manchester United Manager)

He then left, and a few minutes later Rooney came into the room, Khushil couldn't believe his eyes. Rooney went around the room, and when he came to Khushil, he said, 'Khushil, why didn't you tell me that you wanted to meet me? I could have shaved. and would have looked smarter!' It was so thoughtful of the manager and Rooney that they made this possible.

Khushil with Wayne Rooney (Manchester United), March 2016

These are the days which you never forget. All the players were so humble, and made Khushil feel valued and special. They had their own media crew, who took photographs and interviews, and then Khushil's photo and his interview were published in the match day programme that weekend. We were sent a copy of the programme, as a souvenir. I asked Khushil, 'Why don't you share your pictures of the visit to Man Utd with your friends?' He replied, 'I don't like to show off. I am happy that I met them, but I don't like sharing them.'

Then came Easter time. A year previously, it hadn't seemed possible that we would be celebrating this time together. But because of Khushil's strength, we were – together. Khushil picked another holiday, this time it was Turkey. We had a lovely time, celebrating our anniversary on 1st April. We explored Side, and went to lots of local shops. Khushil and I also tried parasailing, for the very first time. It was an amazing experience. Khushil loved it, and after that he tried wind surfing and scuba diving too. For both activities he had 2 days of training, and then on the third day he was ready to start actually windsurfing, and diving. As always, Khushil's confidence and enthusiasm saw him through, helping him to follow his dreams and achieve everything he wanted to.

Khushil in Turkey, April 2016

Before the second radiotherapy treatment in May, even though Khushil himself was suffering from a brain tumour, he took part in the school's charity fund raising event.

Following this, Laura asked me whether Khushil

would be interested in going to an Air Show. As I am sure you've gathered by now, I needed to ask Khushil before answering that question. Laura, the doctors, the consultants and the radiotherapy team all knew that too. So, Laura then asked Khushil – he seemed happy to give it a go. Our experience at the air show was great. We had a good day, but it was a short trip, as Khushil started having headaches after a few hours.

Khushil had always been extremely dedicated towards his studies. He wanted to become a scientist. He wanted to study in Oxford University and was working very hard for that. He achieved the highest marks in all his Science tests, and hence he was chosen for a school trip to Oxford University, on the 6th June. There were only 11 students selected for this trip. He enjoyed this experience a lot, and was very excited at the prospect of studying at Oxford in the future.

Soon, August rolled around, and Khushil wanted to go on another holiday. This time he wanted to go somewhere really crazy. Can you guess? Alaska! Yes, Alaska!! Of all the places. I asked him, 'Are you sure?' and he was very adamant.

We had a couple of appointments with Dr Shankar, to get his approval for us to travel that far. At first he was concerned, but Khushil had a very persuasive way about him. Generally, if he wanted something, then he had a very unique way of making this happen. He would not let us feel as if he was forcing us, or being adamant on those matters. Dr Shankar prescribed a lot of medicines that we needed to take with us, just in case Khushil had any health problems. I carried a whole handbag of medicines with me the whole time we were there, as it was definitely a big risk for us to take. However, all of the stress and visits to Dr Shankar and the visits from nurses beforehand were worth it. As always, Khushil was right. Alaska is like heaven on earth. It really is a place that everyone should visit. It was our once in a lifetime holiday, and the best place we have ever been.

To begin our trip, we travelled to Newark airport on the 19th August. It took roughly 8 hours. Then from Philadelphia to Alaska it took us another 11 hours. By the time we reached Alaska we had passed through four time zones. But the journey was definitely worth it. Alaska takes your breath away. You can see every form of nature, so pure and refreshing. Genuinely, it makes you feel as if you are in heaven. The atmosphere is mesmerising, you can smell the freshness, the beautiful smell of sand, water, and air. Truly divine. We visited Denali National Park, the North Pole (Santa Clause's House), Anchorage, Seward, went to the top of Mt Healy, explored the Kenai Fjords, Alaskan Wildlife and Glacier Cruise, and Fairbanks. We also viewed the Northern Lights, went to the Ice Museum in Fairbanks, and saw whales, seals, otters and other sea life in Seward, and of course how can I forget our visit to Anchorage Zoo.

Khushil selected Alaska because of the wildlife, so he was delighted by all this. In Khushil's own words, 'Feeling very happy after viewing the live glacier and Alaskan marine wildlife. The whales were magnificent, and the sea lions, otters, seals, eagles, falcons and puffins...beyond imagination. It's just not possible to replicate this on camera. It's in my heart.'

Khushil admiring the Alaskan beauty in Seward, August 2016

We spent two wonderful weeks in Alaska. This was Khushil's last holiday, so I am glad it was spent somewhere so incredibly memorable. We received Khushil's scan results in September 2016, after the second round of radiotherapy – the results were not good. The treatment had not made a difference. In November 2016, I noticed that Khushil had started limping on his right leg. I pointed this out to Bhavesh, and he said, 'You worry too much, stop worrying and stop making me worried.' I was adamant though, and absolutely certain that something was wrong. My heart was telling me to call Dr Shankar, so I did. He gave me an appointment immediately, and arranged for another scan. Again, there was a wait between the scan and the results, of two weeks. The same familiar feeling came up, as it did every time we had a scan. My heart would start beating so fast, and my mind was just consumed by worry. Eventually, I got a call, saying the results were ready.

This time I wasn't planning to be brave, and didn't go on my own. Bhavesh came with me. And thank God, because I needed him that day.

After reviewing the results, Dr Shankar said, 'Your instinct was correct, the scan is showing that tumour has started growing again. Unfortunately, I don't have any other treatment this time.' Of course, we were devastated by this, but there was no time for pause. Khushil being Khushil, he decided to join a taekwondo class the very same month. He'd always wanted to learn some form of martial arts, and his admission for Duke of Edinburgh gave him the reason to do so – as one of the requirements was to complete a physical activity. Even though he'd been limping, he excelled, and the teacher told us that if he continued in the same way he'd soon be ready for black belt! Initially, he'd go to classes on Tuesday and Saturday. I used to come home at 5pm, and we'd leave as soon as I got there. Khushil was determined not to be late. He used to say to me, 'If you are not home at 5pm then I will go by bus.' Even with his limp, he was ready to leave an hour early and change two buses just to get there on time.

Khushil with his guru, taekwondo class

Khushil doing his taekwondo moves, April 2017

On top of taekwondo, Khushil was also learning how to play the piano. Again, he excelled at this. He'd written his own music, and I still have all the videos of him playing. He could listen and look at the tutorial of any song once or twice maximum, and then he'd be able to play the tune. As with everything, Khushil managed to get at least one hour of piano practice in every day. He was so dedicated to improvement.

In December 2016, Khushil's health was stable. Apart from the limp, it had not gotten any worse. Bhavesh and I wanted to celebrate Khushil's birthday by throwing a big party again, but Khushil did not want to celebrate. He decided to invite only Himanshubhai and his family, Jalpaben and Hem. That year, we gave him a surprise gift, something which he had wanted since he was 8 years old – a Mont Blanc pen. Khushil was over the moon with this, and the first thing he did was to write in his personal diary with it.

Along with the pen, Khushil also received another gift – a bicycle. Although we knew that he wouldn't be able to ride it, it was important for us to get him this, as he had asked for it. He did try to ride the bicycle a few times, but had a fall. This was just another example of Khushil's determination and resilience. He was willing to give anything a go, no matter how unlikely. We thanked God for giving us another year, which nobody had expected. Not only that, but it had been a great year, full of incredible moments. As you have already seen, as a family we managed to accomplish a huge amount in the short time that we were given together.

On 19th December 2016 I received the best gift of my life. My birthday was on Monday, and on Friday when I came back from work, Khushil said to me, 'I am going to Hem's house to play.' I was a bit surprised by this, but let him go. He went to play with Hem, and then returned back within an hour. I asked him, 'Did you enjoy Hem's house?' and he said that he had lots of fun. On the Monday, Bhavesh and I had taken the day off, so all three of us were home (as Khushil had broken up for the Christmas holidays). Khushil woke up early and got ready. That day, for a change, Bhavesh and Khushil both got ready before me. When I came downstairs, I saw that they had gone and got me a birthday cake. I was extremely happy and surprised. I just couldn't believe it. I said to Khushil, 'When did you get all this done?' and he said, 'Mum, do you remember when I said I was going to Hem's house to play? I went to the cake shop to order the cake for you.' I had tears in my eyes, I was so happy that even in his situation Khushil was still thinking about me. He'd even paid for the cake with his saved money. I was the happiest mum in the world that day, and felt so proud to have Khushil as my son. After my birthday Khushil and I had already planned a surprise party for Bhavesh's birthday, on 24th December!

January 2017 was another stable month, with no significant deterioration. However, when I picked Khushil up from school, I noticed that his limp was getting worse, and he was struggling to make the walk back home. Even though Khushil didn't want me to pick him, as his mum I insisted, so there were times when he had to let me.

Khushil's decision making was always on point, and there were countless moments where he made somewhat surprising decisions, but they always turned out to be correct. One of his best decisions was not to agree to supplementary treatment. Dr Shankar had given us this option, so we made an appointment to meet a specialist at Great Ormond Street. Khushil accompanied me, as he wanted to know what the treatment was about. The specialist told us that the treatment would involve Khushil getting regular blood tests. He wouldn't be able to go on holidays, and he might have to be admitted to hospital. The treatment also meant missing school. I then decided to get another appointment, so that I could ask for the full details of the treatment. The specialist informed us that this was an experimental treatment, so it would restrict Khushil a lot. Khushil's mind was made up early. He didn't want to go ahead, and told me that he was happy with Dr Shankar, and wouldn't be changing doctor. We were happy to go along with Khushil's decision, which was influenced even more by the fact that the supplementary treatment has, until today, a 0% survival rate. We didn't want Khushil to lose his freedom or quality of life.

In the next chapter, I'd like to give you a better insight into

Khushil's personality. Sometimes, I feel as if describing someone's personality in words does not do them justice – and that is certainly the case with Khushil. You have to experience being with that person to get to know them, and understand what makes them great. However, I will do my utmost to show you how Khushil's personality brought out the best not just in us – his parents, but everyone else around him.

Khushil ice skating, August 2017 Philadelphia (USA)

129

The Meaning of Life

Khushil inspired everyone he met, and his bravery, determination and resoluteness continues to inspire people today. He taught us how to live without holding onto resentment or fear. He taught us how to believe in ourselves, and how to make the most of our lives. Life is about how you react to challenges. The way you react is what makes you who you are. Khushil believed, wholeheartedly, that the future is what you make it.

Instead of worrying about what he could not control, Khushil preferred to turn his focus to things that he could create. It's simply not possible to describe Khushil in just one chapter. He had the brain of scientist, and the heart of an angel.

One of the most inspirational things about Khushil, was his understanding nature. He had a way of forgiving people, regardless of what they'd done.

To give you an example, one time when they were playing, Bhavesh accidentally hit Khushil on his nose. The force of the impact was so strong that it brought tears to Khushil's eyes, but even then he didn't say a word. Bhavesh kept on apologising, promising it was a mistake, and trying to make sure Khushil was alright. Khushil very calmly said, 'It's okay, Bhavesh. It was a mistake, I understand.' His voice was so calming and soft. He didn't show anger even for a second. It's not easy for someone to have an attitude like this. We all become frustrated or upset by things in life, and it's almost impossible to contain your emotions all the time.

I think that being as forgiving and understanding as Khushil must come from deep within you. It must be a core part of who you are, as it was him.

From February 2017 onwards, Khushil started facing more and more new challenges. His condition began to deteriorate. However, as things got worse, we began to see the real strength of Khushil. Even more so than before, we were amazed at how someone of such a young age could stay so composed, and show so much compassion for others.

By the start of February, Khushil was struggling to walk. Instead of limping, he was now dragging his foot. Tarak, my brother, and his wife Dhwani came to visit us. Whilst they were here, Bhavesh had to go India to visit his dad, who was not feeling well. He stayed there for three weeks. In the meantime, Khushil looked after me. His tumour had started to grow again, and there were clear signs of progression. When a tumour starts re-growing, there isn't much time left. Anything could happen at any time, so one cannot predict what will happen in the next minute. Tanya had registered with the emergency ambulance service, so that they could be pre-warned if anything happened.

It wasn't easy living this way. I was in a constant state of panic, knowing that I could lose my child any time, and would be unable to do anything to help him. I watched Khushil deteriorate, day by day. There were days where I felt incredibly useless and helpless, but Khushil always told me, 'You are the best, you are very strong. I don't want anything more than what you are doing.' We used to ask him, 'Is there anything that you would like to do, or that you want to do?' His reply was always, 'No, you are the best and you have done everything.' He would sometimes call me near and stroke my cheek and say, 'You are the best.' It was so lovely, and made me feel special.

On the 26th February 2017, Mr Riggs's father-in-law gifted Khushil tickets for the EFL Cup Final (Manchester United Vs Southampton). Khushil and I went to see the match, which Man Utd won. Naturally, he was delighted with this.

As I have previously mentioned, Khushil would push himself to the limit, to try and tolerate as much as possible. He was determined not to let the tumour impact his life. However, there were limits. Dr Shankar had to help persuade Khushil that he should only do taekwondo one day a week, instead of two. Even then, he tried two days a week for a month, until eventually agreeing that because of his leg it wasn't possible. On the 11th March 2017, Khushil got dressed, but then turned to me and said, 'Mum, we won't go to my taekwondo classes. I'll restart when I feel better.' That truly broke my heart. For Khushil to say that really meant he was feeling terrible. Following that, his walking got worse, and he needed crutches to go to school. He was unable to walk without the extra support.

When this happened, everyone at Claremont really came together to make things easier for Khushil. They were fantastic. Mr Riggs and Khushil had agreed that Khushil would have a friend that would help him out whilst at school. Khushil spoke to his friend Mehran, who assisted him when he needed it. Mehran was wonderful to Khushil. He stayed with Khushil from the moment I dropped him off at school, until the end of the day – where he walked Khushil back to my car. He'd even leave his class five minutes early, if they were in different lessons, to make sure that he had lots of time to get Khushil to his next lesson before all the other students started rushing.

It wasn't just Mehran who helped out, but the rest of the students too. There was an agreement between the children who played football that no matter what happened, nobody could push Khushil to get the ball. When I heard about this I thought it was so adorable and thoughtful of them. This is the culture and ethics of Claremont students. All of Khushil's friends would protect him throughout the day, making sure that he was careful on the stairs, and walking slowly with him to match his pace. This wasn't just done for a day, or a week, but it continued right the way through till the last day of school, 19th July 2017.

By March it had become too difficult for us to use the trains when going for Khushil's hospital appointments, so we started driving to the hospital instead. Just to be on the safe side, we always made sure that we picked Khushil up 15 minutes early from school – because the last 15 minutes of the day were always registration time. Khushil wasn't happy about this. He said to Dr Shankar, 'I have missed 15 minutes of school today, so for my next appointment please give me a later time.'

On the 9th April 2017, we visited Longleat Safari. We'd been before, and Khushil absolutely loved it. That day they had an experience day, where Khushil was lucky enough to hold a tarantula, a python and another snake – called Bumblebee. Khushil was so happy. Also, for the first time, Bhavesh and I touched a snake. We did it because Khushil asked us to. Bhavesh got really into it, and even took a spider in his hands. I was extremely scared of carrying the snake, and having it around my neck, but Khushil stood next to me and said, 'Go on, don't worry, I am with you.'

Khushil at Woburn Safari, April 2017

I think in that moment, Bhavesh and I learned to live, in some way. We embraced the unpredictably of the whole thing, put fear to one side, and just let ourselves enjoy the experience. We made the most of the moment, living life Khushil's way, and it felt great. Bhavesh and I were determined not to waste the time we had left with Khushil. Once this was all over, we didn't want to have any regrets, or wish we'd done certain things. So, if Khushil said he wanted to do something, we just did it. We didn't waste time thinking about it, or waiting for tomorrow, as we didn't even know whether we'd have tomorrow. We just ran with it, and tried to give Khushil the best moments possible.

Khushil's deterioration continued. His right hand had started to become weak, to the point where he couldn't write anymore. Mr Riggs made arrangements for Khushil to use an iPad at school, which was so kind of him. Somehow, Khushil still managed to draw. He was brilliant at drawing, even with his weak hand. The last picture he drew was of SpongeBob, which he put on YouTube. It was so good that it got selected for the April 2017 Artist of the Month shortlist! Unfortunately, by the end of the month his right hand had stopped functioning altogether. This meant that he could no longer do certain things, such as going to piano lessons. At every stage, Khushil made the decisions. He decided when to stop his activities, and get on with things that he could actually do, instead of focusing on what he couldn't control. He made all the special arrangements at school himself. He never needed me to go into the school and do it for him, as he felt confident and comfortable enough to speak to Mr Riggs about it.

By the end of the month, Khushil's right leg had also stopped functioning. Still, he refused to use a wheelchair. This created an issue when it came to his Duke of Edinburgh award, as there was a practice expedition taking place very soon. We spoke to Dr Shankar about this, and Khushil convinced Dr Shankar that he would be fine and could cope with the stress of an expedition. Obviously, I had no choice at this point, and Khushil was absolutely determined to go.

Ms Carswell came to my rescue, and assured me that she would personally look after Khushil. She did lots of research on which routes Khushil could take, and the routes which would cause him the minimum difficulty. When I say research, I mean that she actually went to each and every place after school, to make sure that it was safe for Khushil. This is how dedicated the staff at

Claremont were. Ms Carswell would even take pictures of the route, and then email me to keep me informed.

The DofE team also got involved. Ms Carswell had spoken highly about Khushil to them, and they wanted to offer all the support needed in order to help Khushil achieve his goal. When Ms Carswell finally selected the place and the route on which Khushil would take his expedition, she asked me to lend her Khushil's wheelchair, saying that she wanted to try and walk the whole route with it, so that she could be sure of how safe it was.

Until that moment, I had been extremely worried and apprehensive about sending Khushil off for his expedition. After all, I was his mum. However, Ms Carswell's selfless actions made me realise that I needed to put this aside. I needed to support Khushil, and give him the confidence to believe that he could do it.

Unsurprisingly, Khushil threw everything into completing the expedition. He was determined to do every single one of the activities, and made sure that he attended every single after-school meeting relating to DofE. He never once took advantage of his illness. There would be times when other students were standing while doing a particular activity, whilst Khushil had to lean against the wall for support. He still wouldn't sit down, even when they gave him a chair. The group in general was incredibly caring, they really looked after Khushil.

Ultimately, with his determination and perseverance, plus the help of his team and teachers, Khushil successfully completed the practice expedition. That meant that he was eligible to go on the practice expedition, on the 26th and 27th May 2017, which would allow him to go for the qualifying expedition to attain his Bronze Award.

Following this, there was a one-week, half-term holiday. During the half-term Tanya arranged for Khushil to visit "Amazing Animals", where he fed a white tiger, named Brahma. What an experience! He also had a monkey sit on his lap and walk around holding his hand, like a child. This was a lovely day for Khushil, filled with exciting animal encounters. He met lions, tigers, baby alligators, penguins, and even a bear.

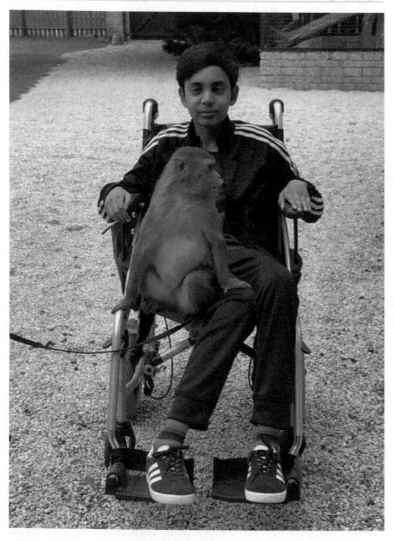

Amazing Animals, Oxfordshire, May 2017

Khushil went back to school on the 6th June. I said to Khushil, 'Please take your wheelchair', as I felt he would need it. He still refused, assuring me that he could manage. Call it mother's instinct, but I was right. Within

139

a couple of hours I got a call from the school, asking me to bring a wheelchair, as Khushil had requested it. That was the first occasion where I met Mr Page. He said to me, 'Don't worry, I will be with him all the time.' He had a very personal touch, and an assuring tone, which made me feel as if Khushil would be safe and looked after.

From that day onwards it was the school's decision that there would always be a teacher with Khushil, who would push his wheelchair around, for safety. Mr Riggs also changed the location of the majority of Khushil's classes, making sure that they were on one floor, so that he could get to them easier. For the few classes which couldn't be changed, Khushil used a special lift.

Mr Riggs asked for us to have a meeting with Ms Thomas, who was the head of the welfare department at the school. The school wanted to meet Khushil's nurse – Tanya, and myself, to ensure that they understood more about Khushil's condition, what to expect, and what to do if certain situations occurred. We were happy to take part in this meeting.

Upon entering the meeting room, and greeting the staff present, we sat down. Mrs Thomas then said, 'I have been doing this job for 30 years. I have never come across anything like this. Generally, parents don't send their children to school in this condition. I think you are very brave. This is the first time that we've had to deal with something like this as a school, so it will be a learning curve for us. We want to help Khushil, but don't know exactly what to do.'

As requested, Tanya was at the meeting, and spoke

very openly and honestly to Mr Riggs and Ms Thomas about what DIPG is, what the survival rate is, and how it affects the patient. After she explained this, there was a moment of silence. I think the teachers were a bit shocked. Then Ms Thomas looked at me and asked, 'Did you know about all of this from the beginning?', to which I said, 'Yes.' I then told her that there was no way I could convince Khushil not to come to school, because this is where he loved being. He loved learning, and nothing I could say would convince him. Mr Riggs agreed with me, and said, 'Even if Khushil was on a stretcher he'd find a way to get into school. I can imagine Ms Taylor pushing him to his lessons. This boy is something else!' Following this, we all agreed a plan moving forward, and made sure that the school had all of the relevant information and contact numbers that they needed.

After the meeting, Mr Riggs took me to one side and said, 'If Khushil wants, then he can come into school a little bit later in the mornings. Or, if he would prefer, he can finish 10-15 minutes early so that he misses the busiest times of school.' I said, 'Mr Riggs, do you want to try and put that proposal to Khushil?' The look on his face was hilarious. We both knew Khushil would never agree to it.

In June, Khushil's condition got worse. He started struggling with his speech, which had become slurred. He could not speak clearly anymore. Still, he found a way to communicate with everyone, and learnt limited sign language. At this point he was getting help with writing his exams, as he couldn't do it himself. However, he still managed to get the highest marks. In Science, he got a mark of 38/40, which was the strongest mark in the year. But, he wasn't happy with that! He said to me, 'My teacher has counted the marks wrong. I have to get this corrected tomorrow. I have to get my 39.'

As June ended, Khushil was due to take his qualifying expedition. Bhavesh and I were both 100% behind him, but we still wanted extra confirmation from Dr Shankar before sending him off. Dr Shankar told us that on this occasion we'd need to give Khushil some medication to take, because without it he wouldn't be able to finish the expedition.

As always, Ms Carswell was phenomenal. She went on the route that Khushil and his group would be taking beforehand, and cut all the overgrown grass and branches which might present a difficulty for Khushil. I have to say that even as a mum, I would never have thought of it. She even made one of the teachers bring along an extra pair of garden shears on the expedition, just in case she'd missed anything! During the expedition, there were a few steps which Khushil was unable to climb. So, one of his team students, Olivia, picked him up and helped him over the stairs. This was so thoughtful and kind of her. The whole group worked very hard, and helped Khushil at every stage.

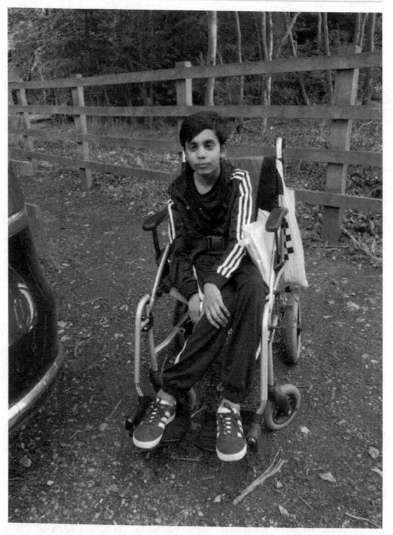

Khushil on his Duke of Edinburgh Expedition, June 2017

Of course, it wasn't without stress, and things didn't go completely smoothly. On the first night I received a call from Ms Carswell, telling me that Khushil was not feeling well, and wanted to speak to me. Bhavesh and I rushed to where they were staying. When we reached Khushil he was freezing. The teachers had him wrapped in four layers, and he was wearing three pairs of socks, along with a couple of scarfs, but he was just so tired. He had no strength at all. We asked for permission to take him away for a bit, and he promptly slept in the car with us the whole night.

The next morning when Khushil woke up, we asked him, 'Would you like to go home, or join your group?' There was no hesitation from Khushil, he wanted to go back and finish the expedition. Ms Carswell was very happy to see Khushil, and with his decision to continue. When I went to drop Khushil back in the morning, I tried to help him get his toothbrush out of his bag. He was not happy with this. He was so independent, even in his condition he wouldn't accept the help. He gave me an absolutely furious look, and then got the toothbrush out himself. Ms Carswell noticed this, and gave me a smile. We both knew that this was just Khushil being Khushil.

Khushil's group was the first group to finish their expedition. As a unit, they were essential in helping Khushil to achieve his Bronze Award, and he was so happy with this. It was just another accomplishment from our remarkable son.

In July, Khushil started having even more difficulties. He was struggling to swallow, and also struggled with going to the toilet. On the 1st July, I had to take him to Northwick Park hospital as a matter of urgency. When we reached there, the hospital staff decided to administer an NG tube – which goes down your nose and into your stomach. Khushil held my hand whilst the nurse was putting in the tube. I put my head to the other side and cried. I couldn't sleep the whole night. Bhavesh came to stay at the hospital too, and the three of us spent the night together. This was really tough, especially for Khushil, but as always he never let his health obstruct him.

Khushil had already completed the physical skills and expedition side of DofE, so all that was left was volunteering. When I went home from the hospital to get ready, Khushil asked me to get his laptop, so that he could complete a poster he'd promised to make – promoting DofE to the next year's participating students. He completed the poster from his bed at Northwick Park Hospital, and then made me email the poster to his teacher. He would not wait until he was discharged. He just kept saying, 'I have to send it today, as promised.' Thankfully, he was then discharged the next day, on the 3rd July. On the 4th July, at 8:30am, he was straight into school, on time. No surprise there.

The 12th July was an award day for all the DofE students. Along with that, they would also be distributing certificates for all of the sections that had been completed. Luckily, we were invited to the award function. Khushil was the first person to have completed all 4 sections, from the entire 27 who participated. There were 14 students who had completed all of the activities, receiving the full Bronze Award – with Khushil being one of them. Following that, Khushil proudly wore his DofE badge on his school uniform jacket, along with a Geographer badge – awarded to him by his geography teacher for his hard work, maximum effort and dedication.

Khushil was extremely proud to have achieved the target that he set. He believed that challenges make life interesting, and overcoming them is what makes life meaningful. He never considered his tumour an obstacle. On the contrary, he overcame the hurdles that the tumour put in his way. He proved everybody wrong, and achieved every single accomplishment that he set out to, in such a short space of time.

On the 5th July, early morning, I got a call from Mr Page. He said to me, 'I am sending you an email, and will copy Khushil in as well.' He had contacted BBC, requesting that Steve Backshall sent a personal video message for Khushil. We listened to the video message over email, and it was the most wonderful thing. Steve said, 'Khushil, I know you are getting good grades and want to become a zoologist. You really are an amazing young man, and you should be so proud of yourself.' Naturally, Khushil was thrilled by this. It was another example of how fantastic Mr Page was – even going to the extent of getting Khushil a personal video message from his idol.

As usual, the 19th July was the last day of Year 9. All the parents got invited to celebrate the year and be a part of the award ceremony. Awards were given for each subject, and then came the big award – Boy of the year and Girl of the year. Khushil received awards for Maths, Geography, and English, plus a Certificate of Excellence for determination and kindness. He also received a Science award from his teacher. All of the awards were important, but the one that Khushil loved the most was the Pupil of the Year award.

Before announcing the Pupil of the Year award, Mr

Riggs gave a speech. Here is what he said:

'It's said that when a country develops, the population starts taking important things for granted. They think that because education is free it has no value.

The majority of you here quash this theory, but one more than the rest.

Never have I known a student with such passion, dedication and commitment to his studies. Yes, he achieves great grades, but more importantly he has made amazing progress. In fact, proving experts' predictions wrong has become something of a habit for him.

What makes this student's achievements even more astounding, is that they have been achieved against a backdrop of real adversity.

The perseverance and determination shown to simply get to school is astonishing, as is the determination to go on and achieve so much. One of his proudest achievements is his success in the Duke of Edinburgh award. Again, many people said this would not be possible. As usual, this stubborn and determined young man ignored them and achieved what he set out to achieve. He is the very definition of mind over matter. If I could bottle his passion, attitude and spirit, I would, and give every student who passes through our gates a bottle. Not to mention my son, every day of his life. He is a total inspiration to me, and to all the students at this school.

The boy of the year for 2017, is Khushil Pandya.'

This is how the day began. I was going through lots of feelings whilst listening to this speech. I was happy, proud, sad, devastated, and helpless. What more could a parent ask for from their child? Khushil excelled in everything, even in the worst possible condition. He was and always will be my pride.

After the ceremony finished, there were so many students, parents, and teachers who came to congratulate Khushil. It was such a proud moment. I was very excited about the awards, and wanted to speak to my parents and my brother and sister. But Khushil told me, 'Mum, calm down. No need to be too excited. Enough of your celebration, get back to work! You have to write your three pages for my science book.' I will explain exactly what this meant in the next section. Anyway, I did start writing, but then had a thought. I said to Khushil, 'Shall we go out for dinner to celebrate?' and he was happy enough to do this. But then he said, 'Since you aren't cooking tonight, you'll have to write five pages!'

Now, let me tell you about the science book. In the middle of year 9, Khushil was given the option to select which subjects he wanted to do at GCSE. He wanted to do triple science, which the school were happy with, since he was so good at the subject. His teacher had told him what books he needed. Khushil was already ahead in science, so he got his books for Physics, Chemistry and Biology, and then started preparing his own little notebook – full of useful info that he would need. He had been doing this since January. Initially, he started writing it, but later on when he started having difficulties I was given the privilege of writing in the book. And believe me when I say this – it wasn't easy for Khushil to let you write in his book. His books were always extremely well looked after. They were colour coded, with beautiful handwriting that most people would envy.

Following the awards ceremony, Khushil's health got even worse. He could hardly speak now, and everything was getting more and more difficult. His mobility had decreased by about 90%. If he wanted to move around the house then Bhavesh had to pick him up. Naturally, we wanted to take him somewhere for the summer holidays. We weren't allowed out of the country, because of the risk to Khushil's health, so we decided to go to

Scotland for a few days.

Dr Shankar reminded us to visit Edinburgh Zoo, as this is the only zoo with red pandas, and Khushil also wanted to see the birds of prey. Tanya made sure that she informed the Edinburgh hospitals, and other hospitals nearby, so that they could be on alert if something happened. She emailed us a letter and gave us contact numbers just in case.

We left on the 25th July. It was a long drive. After enjoying an early dinner at a lovely Indian restaurant, we went back to our hotel and decided to try and relax. Khushil loved the dinner, and said he wanted to go to the same place the next day. Then, after about an hour he complained about a headache. He went to sleep and woke up in the middle of the night, saying that his head was hurting terribly, although he wouldn't let us touch it. We rushed to Edinburgh hospital, and they admitted him straight away and started treatment. Edinburgh hospital then made contact with UCLH and Tanya's team, before admitting Khushil to the ward. The doctors and nurses were all extremely helpful, supportive and kind.

After a while Khushil said that he was feeling okay, but Tanya and her team were in contact with the Edinburgh hospital staff, and it was decided that we should return as soon as possible. We'd driven over 7 hours, and hadn't slept much, so we asked if it was okay for us to stay the night and return the next day. The hospital seemed okay with this, but kept Khushil in overnight just in case.

The next day, we came home. Tanya and Catherine

called us in the morning, and said that they wanted to see us when we returned. They kept in touch throughout the journey, to make sure Khushil was okay. We got home at about 7 in the evening. Tanya and Catherine were already there, waiting to see Khushil. In the space of a day quite a lot had changed, and not in a good way. Tanya checked Khushil's swallowing, and she said that they'd need to administer an NG tube again, so that Khushil could eat. It was hard for me to watch this, since it meant that all Khushil could have was liquid. Following that incident, Khushil tried eating Weetabix for a week, but gave up. All he could have was milk and water. His health started getting worse. He was having even more problems passing urine, sometimes having 15-hour gaps between going for a wee and we had to give him enema for his constipation . He had also completely stopped speaking.

A couple of weeks after we came back from Scotland, we received a parcel addressed to Khushil. When we opened it, we saw that it was a box of gifts for Khushil, from the team of Edinburgh hospital. This was a very emotional moment. Khushil had told them that he really wanted to go to the zoo and see the birds of the prey, so they'd sent him a box of goodies from the zoo gift shop, and a photo of the magnificent owl. In that short stay, the nurses had managed to pick up on the things that Khushil loved most, and sent them all in one lovely little box. It was incredible, and really showcased how good the NHS are.

Even though he was not eating, and his body had become weak, Khushil's mind had not. Dr Shankar was always amazed by Khushil's drive and perseverance, saying, 'Khushil, you are an amazing man. I have worked as a doctor for 25 years, and I've never seen anyone like you. Your attendance at school is over 98%, some people don't go to work because they have a cold! When I have any problem, I just think "What would Khushil do?" and I come out of it in one piece. I like meeting Khushil, he puts things into perspective. You are really lucky to have Khushil as your child. You must be very proud of him.'

By the beginning of August, Khushil was having major difficulties in doing day-to-day activities. He must have done his research, and understood that things were looking bleak, as he said to Bhavesh, 'No matter what happens, don't cry, and make sure you take care of Mum.' Khushil was so mature, even in the face of such enormous adversity. To try and make things easier, Khushil designed his own chart for communication. It was a simple A-Z alphabet chart, which could be used to help him show others what he needed. The speech specialist was surprised with what Khushil had created. She said that this was quite remarkable, and wanted to use it for other children and adults who couldn't communicate. Tanya took a picture of the chart, and said that she would try and get it used at Great Ormond Street, and UCLH.

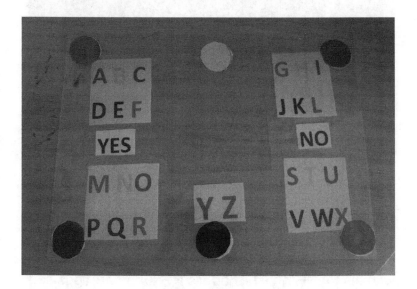

On the 7th August, we completed Khushil's last wish. We visited the Cotswold Falconry Centre, where Khushil could spend time with various birds of prey. There was a surprise waiting for Khushil there. I had rung them, and made special arrangements for Khushil to hold an owl. He absolutely loved this, and we had a great day. The nurses were acutely aware that time was short now, as when I spoke to Tanya about taking Khushil to see the birds, she said, 'Make sure you do it quickly, as this could be his last visit.' After the visit to the Falconry Centre, we went to view the movie "Captain Underpants" with Khushil.

Khushil's last trip to the Cotswold Falconry Centre, August 2017

During the summer holidays, Khushil's teachers visited him a few times. Mr Riggs, Ms Perkins, and Ms Patel all came to see him. I remember when Mr Riggs visited with his family, Khushil had his NG tube. Mr Riggs said, 'Khushil, you will have to teach me how this works, as when you come to school I will need to help you.'

Khushil said, in sign language, 'I can do it myself, but I can teach you now. Let me show you,' and then showed Mr Riggs how it worked.

When Ms Perkins visited, she said to me, 'If you want to go out then I am more than happy to look after Khushil. Any time, any day you have any work, please ring me, and I will come and look after Khushil. I love spending time with him.'

Dr Syed visited Khushil nearly every week during the summer holidays, and she was amazed by Khushil's drawings, his science book, and his other accomplishments. She would look forward to coming for her next visit, as Khushil always had something new to talk about and show her. I had called Chaitali, my sister, to help me. Khushil did not want me to call anyone else. He was only ready to let Chaitali come over. It was very nice of her to come, without her two little daughters, who agreed to stay with their dad in Australia.

At this point, Khushil was unable to perform any activity himself. He needed help in moving his head, hands or any other part of his body. His hands and legs started becoming stiff, so we used to do simple exercises. It was incredibly distressing to watch this. We felt helpless. Every day, we could see him losing. Even in that situation though, Khushil was smiling. He'd still say, 'I'm fine, don't worry.' He had an impossible amount of strength and courage. He knew that I was worried and not eating properly, so he used to make me sit in front of him to make sure that I ate, even while he couldn't. He also got the dietician to make notes of my calorie intake, as well as his own. Even in that situation, Khushil found a way to make me happy. He used to ask me to make a cup of tea, almond and saffron milk, cold coffee, chocolate shake or juices, and then feed him through his NG tube, so that I felt as if I was helping. Obviously, he was not getting any taste, being fed through the tube, but mentally it made me feel as if I was giving him something different from milk or water.

Despite Khushil's best efforts, Bhavesh and I suffered greatly through this. We tried to be strong, of course, but watching our only child suffer was heart breaking and painful. Khushil was more and more uncomfortable with every passing day. He couldn't sleep through the nights, because his eyelids wouldn't close, which meant that his eyes had become dry and burned – even when we applied eye drops to keep them moist. Still, he never complained. The tumour also caused huge amounts of body pain, again Khushil wouldn't verbalise his suffering. He didn't want us to worry.

Even at that stage, Khushil had the inner strength to make decisions. As I've told you lots of times, Khushil had the brain of a scientist. He must have done some research beforehand, because he used to make us put ice on his lips. We all thought this was a great idea, as it would help to keep his mouth moist when he couldn't swallow anything. However, in his phone notes, we found that he had written a research note saying, 'When the brain becomes weak and stops sending messages, you will stop feeling. Therefore, if you put ice on your lips then you won't feel it.' So, this was essentially a way of Khushil checking his own progression, establishing how much time he had left.

Around that time, I noticed that Khushil's breathing pattern had changed. I pointed this out to Tanya, who said, 'That's one of the symptoms of the tumour's progression.' They had a special bed available for Khushil, to make sure he was comfortable. This would be placed in our home, and Tanya had prepared a form that we had to sign, saying that we were happy for Khushil to be at home in his final moments. We were absolutely in favour of this. I didn't want Khushil to die in a hospital, I wanted him to be in my arms, in his beloved home. Obviously, this was a terrible and devastating decision for us to make. No parent should ever have to choose where their child will die, but it was a no brainer.

The days were getting tougher and tougher, but the nights were even tougher than the days. Bhavesh and I couldn't sleep. I used to just sit there the whole night, looking at Khushil. Because his breathing pattern had changed, I was worried about something happening to him while he was sleeping, so I used to check his heartbeat, to make sure it was working throughout the night. I didn't like leaving his side, even to get ready. I would get dressed really quickly, and eat my dinner as fast as possible, to reduce the time spent away from Khushil. Khushil wanted me to be next to him all the time too, and he would get impatient, even if I'd gone out of sight to wash my hands or go to the toilet. Bhavesh and I used to sleep in Khushil's room, on the floor near his bed. At that point, only Khushil's left hand was functioning, and that too was very limited. All he could do was lift his hand and tap it on the bed to call us. We eventually got a bell, with a switch, that he could push whenever he needed us there – on the rare occasions when we left the room.

Still, Khushil never complained. No matter how inconvenient things got, his smile was never affected. He never lost his sense of self-belief, either. One day, Tanya was trying to get Khushil to agree to take his medicine. He didn't want it, so she said to him, 'Khushil, in some matters I am more intelligent than you. You have to listen to me.' Khushil smiled, as usual, and in sign language said, 'Not really, only on a few things.' He was so stubborn, and always wanted things his way. That was why he was able to make the most of the short time he had, and the reason why his impact on everyone around him was so massive. He was and still is an inspirational child. Khushil proved that positivity, determination and resilience can be permanent, no matter the circumstances. You just have to believe.

Khushil at home, August 2017

On the 30th of August, Tanya and Catherine came early in the morning, as they wanted to speak to me and Bhavesh. That day they didn't see Khushil. I could see that they both looked worried and tense. They were and are still attached to Khushil. For them, Khushil was not just a patient. They truly loved him, and treated him as if he was a member of their own family. Tanya and Catherine sat down with us, and then Tanya said, 'I need to talk to you about something really important. It's really difficult for me to say, but Khushil's condition is not looking good. It doesn't look like he's got much time left. As agreed, Khushil will be at home with you. I know Khushil would prefer to be at home rather than in hospital. We will definitely be there to help at every stage. But we would like to suggest that you contact the funeral services, to get some idea of what the procedure is following his death.' It took Tanya a lot of courage to say this, and she was in tears the whole time. Bhavesh and I appreciated her frankness. I asked, 'When you say Khushil has not got much time, what does that mean?' She said, 'Roughly, about 6 weeks.'

This really was a hammer blow. I felt frozen in time. Somehow, even up until that moment, I'd been hoping that a miracle would come around and Khushil would recover, or that the doctors would say they'd made a mistake. Reality hit home. I was going to lose my son.

Tanya and Catherine left without meeting Khushil that day. I don't think they would have been able to face him, and he was clever enough that he would have noticed a change in their behaviour. Bhavesh and I took a while to process the news. However, we both resolved that we wanted to ensure that Khushil did not lose his dignity. Khushil's dignity was paramount to him, and therefore to us too.

On the 2nd of September Khushil had the toughest night so far. He was in a lot of pain, and was restless. He couldn't sleep at all. He was feeling very uncomfortable, and kept on asking us to move his hand, then his leg, and then his face. He just couldn't rest. As his swallowing had stopped completely, it was not possible for his saliva to be swallowed, and that made it worse. At 1.30am we called Tanya to get some help, to make Khushil feel comfortable.

Tanya facetimed us, with Khushil in the room, and told us different things to do. We tried everything, but it was not helping. She was on the call until 3.45am, when finally she had the idea to get Khushil to sleep on his stomach. This helped, somewhat, and he managed to get to sleep for an hour.

The next day was even tougher, and on Sunday Khushil got very worried. He kept pointing at the window, telling me that there was someone there. We just couldn't understand this. We opened his wardrobe and the window, and did everything possible to show him that there was nothing to be worried about, but he just didn't believe us and kept on pointing at the window. He wouldn't let me go anywhere, and made me sit near him. That was the worst we'd ever seen, and we genuinely thought that we would lose him that day. I couldn't control myself, and cried in front of Khushil. Luckily Bhavesh stayed strong. He did cry, but only in a different room. Khushil was surprised by my tears. Even in his condition, he said to me, 'Why are you crying? You should not cry, you are very strong!' Hem and Jalpaben came to visit us later that day, and Khushil asked us to carry him downstairs. He told me to fetch Hem some jelly, and also made sure that it was orange jelly, as 'it tastes better than strawberry jelly, because strawberry jelly tastes like medicine.'

Late Sunday evening, Khushil made me write a question for Tanya, as she was going to visit on Tuesday 5th September. His question was, 'What else is going/might happen (everything)?'

Khushil definitely had some connection with God. That Sunday, he must have spoken to God and said, 'I am not coming with you today. My mum and dad have cried.' I am sure that he knew Bhavesh had cried too. That night, Khushil made me sleep with him on his bed. He just slept through the whole night, which was lovely to see, especially after such a tough day. The next morning he was laughing in his sleep, which made my day. At that point I did not work out that Khushil was trying to make sure we were all happy and laughing with him, before the end of his journey. Even in his situation, he was thinking of me and Bhavesh.

Bhavesh and I woke up early, and got ready, as we had the contractor visiting. We were going to get the lift fixed in our house. The contractor came round and was happy to fix it, making sure it went up from my second reception, through the ceiling, into Khushil's bedroom. He would be starting work from next week. Khushil then woke up, at 10:30am. He was looking quite fresh, and his face had a real shine to it. Honestly, he looked amazing. He had this magical attraction to him, like an aura of sorts. Hayley visited that day, and spent a couple of hours with Khushil. She'd learnt how to use his communication chart by that point, and Khushil seemed in good spirits. When Hayley was leaving, she said to me, 'I know he's not in good condition, but he looks amazing. Even with what he is going through, he has this glow – it's magical. No one would look at Khushil and guess that he was suffering from a brain tumour.'

After Hayley and the nurses left, Mr Riggs came to visit. The last time he visited Khushil, he'd been given three jobs. Khushil had asked Mr Riggs to get his Year 10 timetable, his sets for his subjects, and audio books. Mr Riggs brought the timetables and subject sets, and also told me that he'd made some enquiries about the audio books. When we showed Khushil the timetable, he smiled and then made a funny face, before speaking to me in sign language. Mr Riggs looked at me, confused. I said to him, 'Khushil is telling me that you are going to be his geography teacher, so *I'll* have lots of homework to do.' We all had a good laugh, and when Mr Riggs was leaving he said, 'I'll come again Wednesday, and if you need anything in the meantime then please call me.'

After Mr Riggs left, Khushil told us that he wanted to clean his teeth and have a shower. By 18:50 we had got him ready. Normally, after a shower he came down to watch TV, but that day he said to me, 'Mum, please put me in my bed.' We put Khushil into his favourite trousers, before getting him ready for bed, but he then said to us, 'I want to wear a diaper.' Bhavesh and I were confused by this. Although we had diapers in the house, we'd never had to use them until that point. However, we did as he asked. It was now exactly 19:00. We got Khushil into bed, and he asked me to turn him towards the window. I had him in my arms as I was turning him, and Bhavesh was helping, holding his legs. At 19:05 exactly, Khushil went into a deep sleep. I felt his body become loose and relaxed, and I instantly had a strange feeling inside my body. My heart was beating fast. Mother's instinct, again. I asked Bhavesh to check Khushil, and we tried waking him a few times, but there was no response.

Bhavesh called Tanya immediately. I explained to her what had happened. First of all, she asked me to get some medicine and administer it to Khushil. He did not respond to this. Then she asked me to cut the phone and do a facetime call. As soon as she saw Khushil she told me to go into another room, and said, 'Khushil is in a deep sleep. Trust me, he is at peace, and not in any pain. The reason I asked you to go into a different room is because if Khushil was even 1% awake, he'd listen and understand. He's too clever.' She then said, 'I am not feeling good about this, but he might not wake up. He's gone into a deep sleep, which is likely the result of a seizure. He might wake up in an hour, or in two hours, I can't say. Please spend time with him, cuddle him, and stay with him.'

I cut the phone and sat with Khushil. Bhavesh was not convinced, so he called an ambulance. They arrived very quickly. The first thing they did was to try giving Khushil oxygen. They then called Tanya. She explained to the doctors about the whole situation, and the paperwork that had been completed enabling Khushil to stay at home.

After speaking to Tanya, the ambulance crew took off the oxygen machine and connected Khushil to a heartbeat machine. Bhavesh, Chaitali and I were in the room, whilst the four doctors sat downstairs. Jalpaben and Hem came too. We were all saying our holy prayer, the Gayarti Mantra, to keep Khushil safe. I was holding his hand. I didn't want to let him go. Our house was full of people, but there was a deathly silence, as if in anticipation of what was to come.

The doctors had told me to keep an eye on the machine. They said that if the line on the screen went straight, I should call them. We were all sitting with Khushil, chanting prayers, when I suddenly noticed that the line had changed – it was now straight. Jalpaben called the doctors, who came upstairs and checked the machine. One of them said, 'We're sorry, Mum. Khushil is no more.' The time was 20:40, 4th September 2017.

In that moment, my heart stopped. I lost the light of my life. To say I was in a state of shock would be an understatement. Explaining the pain in words is not possible, and nothing could do justice to my sense of loss. Bhavesh and I have tried to rebuild our lives from that day, but we will never be complete again. There will always be a missing piece of us, of our family, where Khushil once was.

Jalpaben and my sister called our family and friends, asking them to come. The ambulance crew were still there, and they said, 'We are not going to leave until you have family and friends around you.' I called Tanya and requested that we wanted to keep Khushil at home, and not let him go until the morning. She spoke to the ambulance crew, who agreed to this. I was not prepared to let Khushil go to the hospital at that point. I was still hoping that he would wake up, and say, 'Mum, get me some milk or water.' I wanted him to wake up and smile. I sat next to his body the whole night, hoping for him to wake up. It didn't happen. I sat there in disbelief and agony, completely unaware of what was going on in my house. All I remember about that night was that it felt as if my life had come to a standstill, as if I had lost everything. I had lost my hope, my positivity, the very foundation for my existence.

Khushil's Legacy

Khushil was a proud, self-confident person, who brought joy to those around him. He was and is the personification of perseverance, and will be always an inspiration to all. Khushil taught us many good things, one of which was this: 'Life is not about waiting for the storm to pass, but learning to dance in the rain.' In the days following Khushil's death, Claremont gathered testimonials from many of their students who knew Khushil, for Bhavesh and I to read. One of Khushil's classmates had written, *"Your son made me want to try things that I would never have done without him. I just want to say thank you for bringing Khushil into the school."* I received lots of messages from school students praising him, and we got to know lots of things that we didn't before, about Khushil and his conduct. One thing that always struck me, was that Khushil's first day at Claremont High

School was on the 4th September 2014. The last day of his life was on the 4th September 2017. It might be a coincidence, but for me this shows the strength of the bond between Khushil and Claremont.

Throughout his journey, Khushil helped everyone around him, but never expected anything back. He loved to see people succeed, and believed that life is a journey, and not a competition. Khushil helped many people to feel more confident, and not to give up on achieving their dreams. He spoke with confidence and eloquence. His words matched his actions. He proved that everything is possible with the right attitude. He also taught us that discipline is the bridge between your goals and your accomplishments. Another small thing to mention – even at his lowest moment Khushil always wanted as much knowledge as possible. Every day, without fail, (including on the 4th September) he would make a point to read the Daily Mail online, regardless of how he felt.

Khushil's motto, 'No matter how you feel, never give up. Get up and show life that you are stronger than you think, and that you are a warrior' can be applicable to each and every one of us. He never let his physical disability hinder his creativity. Even in his darkest moments, he was in control of his own mind, making his own decisions. He started packing his bags, as if he was preparing for the end of the journey. He himself reduced his milk intake, and ticked things off his list, until the time was ready to begin a new adventure.

The next chapter will provide you with an insight into the impact that Khushil had on others during his lifetime, and even after death. Khushil showed us that what matters most is not living itself, but making the best of your life, and living in the right way.

Life After Death

Like sandalwood, Khushil left his essence everywhere he went. His familiar fragrance of positivity has stayed with every single person he knew. Following Khushil's death, we discovered something quite remarkable. As you know, Bhavesh and I decided not to tell Khushil about the seriousness of his illness. We wanted to protect him. To our surprise, when I read his personal diary, I discovered that he knew from day one about the consequences of the illness. He knew what he'd been diagnosed with, and that there was no coming back. Nobody had told him, he was just clever enough to work it out himself. By not telling us that he knew, he was protecting us. I really couldn't believe it. Somehow, I had underestimated his intelligence. Reading Khushil's diary was a lightbulb moment for us. It gave us the courage to live our lives beyond the 4th September, and to celebrate Khushil's legacy, spreading awareness about DIPG. Now, readers, I want your help. Together, we can advance the research, and ensure that there is a real sense of urgency in doing this. We must find a cure and a reason for this deadly tumour, to save others.

On the morning of the 5th September, we rang the GP, and requested that a doctor visit us. Dr Syed came out to see us, even though it was her day off, and said to me, 'I can assure you, Khushil is in peace now, and looking down on you.' She checked Khushil over, and got some paperwork ready. We then needed to decide on which funeral service to use. We eventually settled on Co-Op Funeralcare. They made me feel as if they were going to take care of Khushil, and told me that they would come at 1430, pick him up and take him to the chapel – where he would be looked after.

Whilst we waited for them to arrive, I sat next to Khushil. I just kept expecting him to get up and say, 'Come on, Mum, let's get ready.' Even though he had just died, he looked amazing, and there was still a glow to his face. I kept on praying, hoping that he would wake up. Then, someone said, 'The Funeralcare people have arrived.' I froze. I couldn't deal with it. I was not ready to let Khushil go, but of course I had to. Following that, I was asked to complete some paperwork. This was a terrible moment, and I pray that no mother reading this has to go through the same thing. I wanted to select the flowers for Khushil's wedding, and to help decorate his wedding reception, just as I had selected his baby bed and his toys. No mother should ever have to select the coffin in which they will lay her son, nor the flowers that will be used at the funeral. This was the hardest and most difficult piece of paper I have ever had to sign. My hands were shaking, and I had a blank moment, where I didn't remember anything. I felt as if I was entering into a black hole, where you cannot see anything, and nothing makes sense. All I wanted to do was cry and cry.

After I signed the paperwork, they asked me, 'When would you like the funeral to take place?' I was not ready to make that decision, mentally it was too much. With this in mind, the family decided that it would be best to hold the funeral on Saturday, as Bhavikbhai and Ketanbhai were going to travel to London that Friday.

Khushil was due to be taken to the Watford chapel, where he would rest until the following day, and would then be brought to Church Lane chapel on Thursday. When Charlotte, who was in charge of this process, asked whether we wanted to visit him, Bhavesh instantly said yes, but I was a bit hesitant. I thought that Khushil might look completely different, and that this would be difficult to deal with. But Bhavesh was adamant, and so we arranged for Charlotte to ring us once Khushil arrived at the chapel.

From Tuesday onwards, we had requested a priest to come to our house, to perform the Bhagwat Gita Path, until Saturday. All of our friends and family had taken time off work, and were with us the whole time, helping us to get through it. We all had dinner together. We decided not to mourn, and instead to remember the strength that Khushil showed. We wanted to celebrate his life.

On Wednesday, we went to give Charlotte some of Khushil's clothes. As I've mentioned, Khushil was very particular in what he wore, and how he had his hair done. His favourite brand was Ralph Lauren Polo, and he would only go to Hobmans, a local barbers, for his haircut. Charlotte took lots of notes, taking details on everything from how Khushil liked to dress, to the knots on his shoelaces.

On Thursday, we went to visit Khushil. I was surprised to see that Charlotte had taken care of every single little detail in getting Khushil ready. She was obviously fantastic at her job. Khushil seemed really peaceful, as if he was smiling at me and saying, 'Mum, I am fine.'

Charlotte had put a big teddy bear in the room, along with some beautiful flowers and candles. I stood there looking at Khushil, and immediately I was hoping that he would wake up and say, 'Mum, let's go.' He looked so handsome and amazing. It was almost impossible to believe that he was gone.

When we were leaving, Charlotte said to me, 'Don't worry, he is at peace and I will look after him. Khushil is a very good boy and looks like he loved his school.' My motherly instinct told me that Charlotte was looking after him, and that's why he was smiling when I saw him. My heart was no longer scared or worried. I had peace of mind that he was in a good place.

I'm extremely grateful to Bhavesh for making the decision to go and visit Khushil at the chapel. In hindsight, I think this was a really important moment for us, and we would sincerely have regretted it if we hadn't been to see him. After visiting the chapel, Bhavesh and I made the decision that we would make a conscious effort to donate to charity, to spread awareness and raise funds for research on DIPG. With this in mind, we set up a link on JustGiving, where people can donate. Visit the following link for more information: https://thekhushilpandyafund.org/.

On Friday, Bhavikbhai and Ketanbhai arrived. As you know, my sister Chaitali was already there. Even though she is younger than me, she has been an absolute rock. Chaitali was my strongest pillar of support, and provided a backbone for me at the time. She looked after us like a mum. I cannot thank her enough, and wouldn't want to, as I would prefer to be in debt to her for the rest of my life. Chaitali sacrificed time with her own children, leaving them with their dad in Australia, so that she could comfort me over the loss of mine. Love you Chaitali!

After Bhavikbhai and Ketanbhai had arrived, we went to visit Khushil. They were stunned by how Khushil looked. He looked exactly the same as when Bhavesh and I went to see him…well actually that's a lie, he looked even smarter and somehow more handsome. To my surprise, Claremont had contacted the Funeralcare service, and had honoured Khushil by sending him the shield logo of the school, made up of flowers. They got these done with the same florist who was making the flowers for the coffin, so that it kept the same theme and colours. They knew that Khushil was very particular about everything, and therefore would have appreciated this.

On Friday morning, the funeral director came to our house, to do some risk assessment. Her name was Alison. I clearly remember the first thing she said to me, which was, 'You are so lucky. I just met Khushil, he is a lovely boy, and his eyelashes are so nice.' Straight away, I felt as if she genuinely cared about what she was doing. This wasn't just a job to her. We'd specifically requested that Khushil would pass by Claremont School, before going to the crematorium. Alison was very supportive, and made me feel as if Khushil would be looked after in just the right way. She gave us a full breakdown of the schedule, explaining to me that Khushil would be arriving at home at 9am for the religious rituals, then he'd return to the chapel for 10:45am. Following that, he'd go past the school gates at 11:15am. She reassured me multiple times that they would look after Khushil, and make sure he was comfortable.

At that moment, I have no words to describe how I felt at that moment. It was surreal. I'd never dreamed of being in that situation, discussing my son's funeral…but there I was.

After Alison left, we then went to visit Khushil again. I couldn't wait to see him and talk to him. His smile made me forget the pain I was going through. Whenever I went to see him, I struggled to leave. It felt strange to be visiting my own child, and then coming back without him. Every visit, leaving became more and more difficult. I didn't want time to pass. I wanted it to stop, so that Saturday would never come, and I could just stay there with my son.

Mr Riggs visited us that day, to see how we were doing, and also to get the schedule for the funeral – as I had mentioned to him that we'd be passing the school before going to the crematorium. He was happy with the allotted timeframe.

That week, my house was full of people, but somehow it felt so empty. It had lost its life. It didn't even feel like my home anymore, just a place where I stayed. I was alive, but I would never be the same as before. A part of me had changed, permanently. I fought with God a lot in that week, asking why he did this. I blamed Him. I demanded answers, asking him, 'If you wanted someone from my family, why not me?'

I couldn't sleep the whole night on Friday, and neither

did Bhavesh. To be honest, both of us had barely slept since the 4th. Bhavesh stayed beside me though, and was strong for me. He never shared how he felt, thinking that I wouldn't be able to take any more stress. One of the most difficult things we had to do, was to prepare a speech for the funeral, describing Khushil. We realised that ultimately there was no one speech which could really summarise our perfect son, but we put something together anyway, hoping that it would do justice to Khushil and his strength, determination and positive attitude.

On the day of the funeral, we had specifically told everyone not to wear white. Even though this was the tradition of our religion, Khushil lived a life of colour, confidence and positivity. He spread smiles and happiness around him wherever he went. We wanted the funeral to reflect this. Everyone was instructed to wear colourful clothes.

That morning my heart had a very strange feel to it. It was the last time we'd see Khushil in the flesh, and that scared me. When Khushil left the chapel, my heart told me that he was coming, and when he reached our house I could feel his presence. I opened the door and at that exact moment the hearse arrived – my heart knew exactly where Khushil was. Very carefully, and with the utmost respect, Khushil was brought into the house so that we could do our rituals. When they opened the coffin cover, I couldn't take my eyes off him. He looked magnificent. He still had the glow and shine on his face, and it mesmerised every person in the room. It was a glow of spiritual beauty, as if he was in a deep sleep and would wake up any second. In that moment, I was lost. I couldn't feel the presence of anyone else around me. It was just me and Khushil. I wanted it to stay like that, and never wanted that moment to pass.

That two hours went extremely quick. We were hoping that the Neasden Temple Saints would come to bless Khushil, which they did, and they performed the final rituals. All of Khushil's teachers from Claremont attended the rituals too. They stayed until all the rituals were completed and then left at 10:45am. Soon after that, Alison arrived, to proceed to Hendon crematorium.

Once she arrived, Alison said sensitively, 'Mum, please let me know if you are okay for us to close the coffin. Once we close it, we won't be able to open again. Please take your time and take a last look at Khushil.' Bhavesh and I asked for a few minutes alone with Khushil. I cried so much, I just couldn't control myself. My heart was so full of pain. I had finally realised that now there was no hope of Khushil waking up and talking to me. I was in a moment that I had never dreamed I'd experience. I begged God to put things back to how they were, before all of this happened. Those few minutes with Khushil went by slowly. We felt every single second. Finally, we were ready. The coffin was shut.

As planned, we went to the school first. We were there at exactly 11:15am. Khushil had never been late in his whole life, so we weren't going to let him down. When we reached the gates, we saw that all of the students from Khushil's year group had come to see him off, wearing their school uniform. The students and teachers had lined up from the starting corner of the school, all the way to the end of the road. This was such an emotional moment, and it really showed us the respect that Khushil had earned in his short but accomplished life. Hem decided to go with the hearse, and was joined by Chaitali and Alison. This was a very brave decision from Hem, and it showed just how much he loved Khushil. We felt honoured and respected by his choice. By the time we reached the crematorium, all of the teachers were waiting for us outside.

Initially we were told that we would need six people to lift the coffin, bringing it into the crematorium. Mr Riggs and Mr Page kindly agreed to help us. However, when we got there, instead of six people we had many others who wanted to help, to show Khushil the love and honour that he deserved. I had requested that Khushil be taken in first, and then the rest of us would follow him – he had always been the boss throughout his life, and that wasn't going to change now. The church was absolutely packed, I really had not imagined that there would be that many people attending. Catherine attended the funeral, and in honour of Khushil, Tanya took her dogs (which Khushil loved) for a walk at the same time as the service.

The ceremony started with a religious offering, followed by the speech from the priest. Our priest, Pravinbhai, had never met Khushil before, but his speech was really touching and thoughtful. Following that, Mr Riggs spoke, and was followed by our friends and family. Then it was our turn. All of the speeches were highly emotional, and focused on Khushil's positivity, his smile, his attitude, determination and good nature. Above all, they focused on the way that Khushil impacted all of our lives, to such an incredible extent.

After all the speeches, it was time. This was the moment I had really been dreading. As a parent, you are hardwired to protect your child at any cost. You will put yourself in front of danger for them, without batting an eyelid. Now, I was putting my child into the flames. I gathered all of my courage, and went up to the front with Bhavesh and Chaitali. I touched the coffin for the last time, and kissed it for good luck. I just kept asking myself, 'Why did this happen?' I didn't want my son to go into that inferno, to be lost forever. I'd been happy, so happy, just being a normal mum. We'd never asked for any of this. Please, readers, help me make a difference. Help me take the fight to the dreadful illness of DIPG. No other mum should have to suffer as I did.

All of our family members, plus Bhavesh and I, went into the room to perform the final ritual. As soon as they switched on the conveyor belt, my heart stopped. My body went into shock. It was unbearable. At that moment, I was thinking, 'Why can't I go with Khushil?' I couldn't get over the fact that I hadn't been able to save him. He went through all that pain, and passed away in front of my eyes. I felt helpless. Even today, I close my eyes and I can still picture that dreadful scene, as if it's happening right now. Luckily, Bhavesh and Chaitali were there, by my side, holding my hand. He gave me the strength to get through it.

After the ceremony Mr Riggs and all the teachers that had attended were there to give us moral support. Mr Riggs was personally thanking everyone who gave a speech. As I've mentioned, Mr Riggs is like family to us. He even brought along his wife and his son. All of the teachers waited until everyone else had left, then told me some stories about Khushil that I didn't know. For example, one of his teachers told me that Khushil used to decide the route on which they would use to go from one class to another, and if she took a different route then that wouldn't be allowed! One of his science teachers told me that, on one occasion, she helped Khushil to write his science test. Once he'd finished the test, he asked for the answer paper, to check whether the teacher had written the answers correctly! Khushil being Khushil, he was a perfectionist, and was always trying hard to get the very best result possible.

At this moment, if I was to summarise Khushil's life, I would say that there is one painting which does an excellent job. The painting is titled "The Light of the World", and the artist was William Holman Hunt, who finished the work in 1853. The painting shows Jesus, preparing to knock on a door which has been closed for a very long time. All around the door there are weeds and uncut grass. The door represents revelation: "Behold, I stand at the door and knock; if any may hear My voice, and open the door, I will come into him, and will sup with him, and he with Me."

The door in the painting has no handle, and can therefore only be opened only from the inside. Essentially, it represents "the obstinately shut mind".

Khushil showed us that if we open the door, there is no limit to what we can do. Once we open the door, we can make an impact on the lives of others, and make the world a better place. Khushil's mind had a different way of looking at life, and his smile had the power to change the world. It had the ability to make everyone around him feel positive. Khushil taught us that when we reach a point where we can't control what is happening, the best thing you can do is to control the way you respond to the situation. When you can do this, you will have real power. Instead of ignoring the negatives, Khushil simply made it his aim to overcome them. In line with this, one of his schoolmates sent us an ancient Japanese quote, which I believe very accurately sums up Khushil. Here is what it said:

"The Devil once whispered to a warrior, you will never make it through the storm. Days later, the warrior whispered to the Devil, 'I am the storm.'"

After the funeral we went to India, as there were religious rituals which needed to be performed. These would ensure Khushil's peaceful transition, from this world to heaven. We held a Bhajan Sandhya (religious songs ceremony) to pay tribute to Khushil. This was the first time in my community where such an event had been Organised. Normally there is a ceremony where people come for few minutes, mourn, and then return home. But we did not want to mourn. We wanted to follow in Khushil's footsteps. Hence we invited a famous humourist to come along too, named Shahdbuddhin Rathod. Shahdbuddhin is not just a humourist, but a highly respected man, who is known for his intelligence, social values, and ability to bring the community together. We felt honoured that he chose to attend. Khushil had always wanted to meet him, but we had been unable to fulfil this wish, so his attending the event made us feel as if we'd made up for that, somewhat.

When we arrived in India, we were informed by Bhavesh's family that Bhavesh would not be able to perform the rituals, because of the rules surrounding our culture. We didn't agree with this. After all, who could be better than Bhavesh to perform the rituals? There could be no other person with the same feelings, love and respect for all the rituals, having held Khushil so close to his heart. Khushil once asked Bhavesh, 'Who told you that we have to do things this way? Who wrote the laws of our culture?' Bhavesh replied, 'My mum', to which Khushil said, 'Where is it written that we cannot cut nails on a Saturday, or at night? What's the reason behind this?' He would not accept anything unless it made sense logically. His scientist brain wouldn't allow for it. After that, Bhavesh used to say to Khushil, 'I have followed the ways of our culture, but you don't have to if you don't agree.' Now, suddenly, Bhavesh and I found ourselves in the same situation. And we'd learned from Khushil.

Bhavesh and I decided not to accept the decision made by Bhavesh's family. As far as we were concerned, Bhavesh was perfect for the ritual, and that was that. The only explanation they gave was, 'Because Bhavesh is his dad, he cannot.' We certainly weren't going to let a rule as silly as that stop us, and Bhavesh ultimately performed all of the rituals perfectly. There really was no one better to do them. Not only was Bhavesh Khushil's dad, but he was his best friend. We gave Khushil the send-off that he deserved, but we did it our way – and I know he would have been proud of that.

Whilst we were in India, Khushil's best friend posted a message on his Instagram. It was written after he'd attended Khushil's funeral, with his dad. Here is what it said:

"I just went to a funeral. I knew my best friend since we were 5…And he could do anything, mathematician, artist, pianist, scientist, philosopher, martial artist and most importantly… As we used to explore the garden in Roe Green he used to tell me all about each animal/bug that we saw… The best zoologist the world has ever seen in my eyes. THE NEXT STEVE BACKSHALL. He lives an 80 year old person's life in 14… If you're gonna be happy then you gotta accept the fact everyone dies, but their mark on the earth is forever. Buddha said nothing is permanent, but that got me thinking… Will the truth in that statement be permanent then? Meh, no point asking questions unanswerable. But life has an amazing thing in it we all know is real, Happiness. Which is what Khushil means by the way might as well feel it a lot more if it feels good right? Khushil would want us to anyway…"

When we came back from India, I received a letter in the name of Kelly – from my work. To my great surprise, it was a certificate, saying that Kelly had registered a star in Khushil's name. There was also an email from Tanya, which had a personal video message from Novak Djokovic, and he also posted a signed t-shirt for Khushil! And after all that, there was even more. Claremont had arranged an assembly in memory of Khushil, which took place on the 11th October. We were honoured to be a part of this. When the assembly started, Khushil's favourite songs were played on the piano. Various students played different songs, using different instruments, and they had also written a poem for Khushil. Then, Hem gave a speech, which was extremely touching. After the assembly, Bhavesh and I had an hour-long meeting with all of the teachers. They gave us a message book, which had lots and lots of lovely and beautiful messages from students and staff. There wasn't enough space in the book for everyone to write what they wanted to say, so I also got posters with messages on! I couldn't possibly have asked for anything more, it was wonderful. Khushil's conscientiousness, positivity and optimism had impacted everyone at that school, and the outpouring of love and respect was testament to that. Claremont High School were incredible to us, and still are today.

Below are just a few messages from the book and the posters:

"Those We love don't go away, they walk besides us everyday......Unseen, unheard, but always near, still loved, still missed and very dear."

"A fulfilled 14 years of life is just as precious as 100 years of Life."

"I know your life was difficult but you didn't let that stop you from doing the things you love, this is why you are my inspiration to succeed in the thing I love, like you did. Thank You."

"The one of a million things that stood out from his was

his positive attitude towards school. I sat next to him in History every lesson for a year, he was always open to help me out during lessons. Even when he wasn't at his best health. I'd often help him with the work too but we would always find a way to reverse that. Khushil was a spark of hope, a lightness in the darkest times. I wish I could thank him, but now I personally want to thank you..."

"You don't know me but the day you died it broke my heart, I don't like school but you do, I made a promise to myself the day you died I would love school and listen to my teachers."

"Forever lost but never forgotten and always loved."

"You always saw the best in everything and everyone. You always put on a brave smile and tried to do everything yourself, I admire you for that. You will never be forgotten"

"I was in his science class and he knew everything"

"I remember when I used to sit next to you in Maths back in Year 8 and you used to help me with everting, RIP little man :)"

"He was a brave and kind soul, I remember our French lessons together, it was memorable and he was always willing to learn."

"I remember our PSHE lessons together and how we used to debate our points."

"Khushil loved to play table tennis with us and we shared many laughs."

"I sat next to Khushil in Geography and he would always help me when I need help even though he hasn't done the question! Khushil was such a nice, brave person and he was always be part of us."

"A good memory I have of Khushil of when we were in Year 9 Science we were getting our test scores back, I didn't know Khushil well but he had one of the highest scores in the class, it surprised me the motivation he had, he would always work hard no matter what. He was a model for all of us, to be grateful for what we have."

"Khushil and I used to sit together in English, and we were said to act out the Romeo & Juliet play with a few other people."

"Khushil always put other people first and he was a caring person. Every time he came to school, when anyone is sad, he put a smile on our face."

"Khushil always participated in class and was one of the smartest people there. He was a very inspirational person full of compassion."

"You inspired me and unlocked my growth mind set. Even though we weren't friends, I now regret not knowing you".

"Khushil was always such a great friend. The memories we shared were truly amazing. He was generous, smart and very competitive. Whenever I needed help, I would turn to him first as he always shares his wisdom. He will be missed."

"**Set 1C Buddy** So excited to be in the same set as you in Year 10."

"He was in my art class in Year 9. He was a very good artist and he was always polite."

"Khushil Believed He Could So He Did."

"Even though our meeting was brief your personality has left a deep print on me. You conquered each and every day with a smile and jokes!! I Know you are somewhere, where you 're shining and you're being the angel I know you are!" This was the message written by a student from **year 11**.

These messages that you have just read are just a small sample of what was in the message book and posters. Every single message was written from the heart, sincerely, and it makes me proud and emotional every time I look over them. Unfortunately, I am not able to include all of the messages, as that would be enough to fill an entire book!

There was another lovely poem sent to me, by Marcia Fowlin. It was written by the mother of Khushil's friend, Brandon:

Khushil

How many of us can truly say

That we've touched many lives in a special way?

I know someone who resides in such a glory.

His name is Khushil Pandya, and this is his story.

Wherever he went he drew an appreciative gaze,

Awestruck teachers, Steve Backshall's praise,

Illness struck, and people told him he couldn't.

But despite protestations, listen he wouldn't

"Duke of Edinburgh Award? That's not for you-

Can't you find something easier to do?"

Khushil ignored their advice. He had a vision.

He dumbfounded naysayers and completed his mission.

His grades were stellar, he loved to learn,

A desire for knowledge would his eyes burn,

He loved Claremont and he was duly awarded,

His steely determination had to be rewarded.

My heart is heavy, but I truly know.

Khushil now basks in a celestial glow.

And in some dimension we cannot see

He's happily studying zoology

Thousands of animals are in his thrall,

Species unknown to man, great and small.

He puts down his pen and someone ruffles his hair,

George Best in his heyday is standing there.

George tells him about the United of old,

The Man U stalwarts who broke the mould,

In an angel-filled stadium the two of them play.

Then after the game they watch Match of the Day.

Namrata and Bhavesh, how proud you must be

Of Khushil's inspirational legacy?

You lit the spark, he carried the flame

We're all the better for knowing him, we'll never be the
same.

Whenever life's challenges stare me in the face'

I stare back defiantly, with dignity and grace;

Because I know just what Khushil would do:

He'd say "I've nothing to fear from you".

I know, right? Absolutely incredible. As if all this didn't make us feel proud enough, we were then invited back to Claremont on the 14th November, for the Duke of Edinburgh Awards. I had been waiting for this day, and I had a feeling it was going to be really memorable and emotional. The Duke of Edinburgh award had been Khushil's pride and joy, and he wore the badge with the utmost pleasure and pride. We were allowed to invite our family and friends along too, which was great.

The evening started with a welcome song, "Let Me Go Home". This was one of Khushil's favourites, and throughout the evening various students played songs to pay tribute to Khushil. Ms Carswell requested that I bring along a picture of Khushil, which was then placed in the centre of the room. It really felt like the evening had been dedicated to Khushil, like a tribute to his legacy.

There were a huge number of people in attendance that night. This included Andrew Lapthrone, a Paralympic tennis player, all of the Claremont teachers, and Amanda – the head of the Duke of Edinburgh initiative at Claremont. Various awards were given out over the course of the night, until finally there was just one left. The final award was introduced as 'The Khushil Pandya Most Inspirational Award', and guess who was the first person to receive the award? That's right, Khushil Pandya himself. Bhavesh and I were so honoured by this. We went up and collected the award on Khushil's behalf. We had no words to say, just lots of tears of pride, happiness and sorrow. It was a really emotional night.

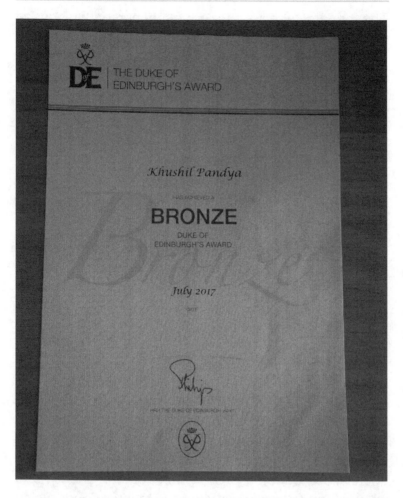

On the 8th December, we celebrated Khushil's birthday at Claremont, with all of his teachers present, and then had a little party at home to celebrate his fantastic spirit and determination. We had already decided that we would celebrate every single birthday as if Khushil was there with us. Khushil represented happiness – the type of happiness which will always be with us. Not only that, but Khushil represented tenacity, and fighting spirit.

The general survival period for a person diagnosed with DIPG is 6-9 months. Khushil lived for 2 years and 6 months. He fought a long and painful battle with the tumour, and the tumour could not break him. Khushil could not be broken. He lived life on his own terms, and he alone made the decision on when he would leave this earth. When Khushil was with us, Bhavesh and I were constantly told by others 'you parents are so strong', but now we realise that it wasn't us who was strong. It was Khushil who kept us going, and still does today. We were blessed, truly.

As I've explained, the reason I wrote this book was because I wanted to keep Khushil's legacy alive, and pass his positive attitude on to as many people as possible. I hope that after reading this book some of this has rubbed off on you.

More than just spreading positivity, I also want to raise awareness about DIPG. If you are a parent, then you will understand the depth of a mother's love for her child. We must come together to prevent others from losing their children, and going through the unimaginable pain that Bhavesh and I have suffered. The proceeds from this book will be donated to the Brain Tumour Charity, and will also go towards the Khushil Pandya Fund, which provides funds for research on DIPG. As I've mentioned, you can donate to our charity page on JustGiving.com, by searching "The Khushil Pandya Fund". Every little helps! Your contribution will help children everywhere to live longer. If everyone makes an effort, we really can achieve our target, and find a cure for DIPG.

Before I finish writing, all I want to say is this:

Khushil, we love you, and we are extremely proud of you. We are so proud to be known as Khushil's parents, and to live up to your name is an honour. We might never be able to reach your standards, but you taught us that failure is not an option. If you believe in yourself, and are determined to achieve your goals, anything is possible. Your life was a blessing, your memory is a treasure, and we love you beyond words.

Keep smiling, keep believing.

I have never got a chance to say it properly, but I would like you to know, Bhavesh, that you are the best life partner anyone could ask for. You have been my rock. Although the front cover has my name on it, this was only possible because of you. I would not have been able to complete this without Khushil's strength, and your support. You are the best husband, friend, philosopher, and critic. I am who I am because of you. Just as Khushil is my heartbeat, you are my breath. You are the reason for my existence, and Khushil is the meaning behind everything that I do. Thanks for everything, and most importantly for being the best part of my life along with Khushil. Love you!

Now, I leave you with the words of those who knew and loved Khushil – our friends and family.

Reminisce

(Courtesy of Roshnee)

Chaitali

I still remember dawn of 8th December, 2002…when our family was gifted the first child/grandchild.

Big eyes and nice black hair, he was an angel, Head to Toe…

Grandpa called him "Chhotu" and I used to give him at least 10 different names during the day.

He was the Royal of the family and I used to "Brand" all his personal belongings with Tarak. Well, to the extent that his nappies also had his name on it.

Grandma was just so busy in his service, which surely showed that he was dearer to her than any of us.

And he was named KHUSHIL…happiness of our family.

As he grew up, I started telling Namrata that he should be my son, as he had all my qualities (I just love to brag about being his "Masi").

He is a Kind little man and is always Honest in his opinion. His Unique characteristics make everyone fall in love with him. Although he has always been Shy in talking to girls, his Hallowed personality put him in popularity everywhere. His Intelligence sets him on the top of popularity chart. Love You Khushil.

I went to London in September 2015 with my family,

as I wanted my daughters to spend some memorable time with Khushil. Although they have lived in different countries, Khushil and my daughters (Mahi and Krupa) shared the special bond of brother-sister relationships. They always had fun with riddles and funny jokes over Skype/Facetime. Krupa used to call him "Khuchi bhaiya" in her toddler tone.

Luckily, I was the one chosen (by him) with whom he would spend the most precious days of his life. So, I went to London again in August 2017. This time it was only me. There was lots of hope, and I just wanted to cherish those days with him. Well, Khushil is the BOSS, so he put me straight into exercise (although he could not speak at that time, his eyes were enough to make me lose my calories).

We shared a common love for books. I knew how much he loved his books. They were like treasures to him. He has his particular way of organising his room and his books. Knowing how much he loved them, I was of course tempted to take one of his books, just for reading. So, one day I took one of his books to read, just while he was out of the room. All of a sudden, Namrata came to me and told me that Khushil was on the way back after his shower. I ran back to his room as fast as I could, put the book back exactly where it was, and released my breath! Namrata was impressed with my speed…and couldn't contain her laughter.

Believe it or not, I actually gained expertise in understanding Khushil's communication chart. It was the most effective way of communication….we were totally in his control, and it created the best memories for me. He was quite vigilant about his condition and the treatment. He insisted on checking the expiry dates of all new medicine given to him (which is remarkable when you are able to communicate using your eyes).

I met many of Khushil's teachers whilst he was ill, and I could not be proud enough of my Khushil after listening to their respectful and positive comments. He was an inspiration to many students around him. His sheer commitment to education never faded, even in adverse physical conditions. More than 99% school attendance on wheelchair is impossible to achieve. Well, it was Khushil's hobby to make possible the impossible. Whilst he was ill, he met many of the legends who inspired him in life, but he himself has become an idol for many of those who met him.

I still remember the 4th September. He was shining like a star. He was at his best on that day. On the 3rd September, he pointed to the photo of Lord Swaminarayan from the Neasden Temple, right in front of our eyes the whole time. He was showing us the ultimate liberation of his soul.

Thank you, Khushil, for showing us how to live our lives – simply by living your own.

Shantaba, Manish and Priya

We are the Patels, one of the closest family friends of the Pandya family. There are five of us in total, but Khushil was closest to my mum, who he called, 'Shanta-ba' – 'ba' meaning grandmother.

We first encountered the Pandya family on the 7th May 2004, when my parents were flying back from India. Coincidentally, the Pandya family were also on board. Little did we know that this was going to be the start of a beautiful, lifelong relationship. My mother had taken notice of the pushchair that Khushil was travelling in. A few months later, she met Khushil and his mum on the local high street, where she recognised the same pushchair. This was the icebreaker. From then on, we became friends, and a special bond was formed with Khushil. Over time, Khushil would visit frequently, and through his pre-school, nursery and primary schooling, he would visit our house almost daily. Our house was only a few doors away from his school.

We have fond memories of Khushil. His inquisitive nature was most captivating. This curiosity only grew with age, and in particular was geared towards dinosaurs, spiders and reptiles! From an early age he would watch back-to-back wildlife documentaries by Steve Backshall (his hero), instead of watching cartoons. Many times, he would educate me with random facts like 'this is a Tyrannosaurus rex and it weighed this much and had this many teeth'. He really was an extraordinary child, both spiritually and mentally. At times his behaviour was so grown up, it was hard to believe he was only 10!

We all know how obedient Khushil was. One day, when I returned from work, Khushil ran up to me and asked, 'Uncle, can I go to the loo?' I thought about this for a second. Did he really need permission to ask for this? He knew us so well by that point, and there were no formalities. He was right at home, so there was no need for him to ask. I thought, 'Let's test him, and see if he really means it.' So I told Khushil, 'No, you cannot go for a wee,' and then made my way upstairs to freshen up. Obviously, I did not expect him to follow my instructions. At most, I expected him to go and ask someone else for permission, and then use the bathroom.

Almost 10 minutes later, I came downstairs to find Khushil still standing there waiting for a permission. Who would have thought that this little boy would take me so seriously? I asked him 'Why are you still standing here?' and his reply was 'You told me not to go'. I immediately gave him permission, and the speed at which Khushil went running towards the bathroom would have put Usain Bolt on the second podium.

Other than this speedy performance, his personality was quite the opposite – very calm and collected, very quiet. If he was watching TV, you would often not realise he was even in the room.

From an early age, Khushil always wiped his mouth with my mum's saree (Indian traditional female garment with a drape over the shoulder). He always used the drape to dry his hands and mouth, the hand towel never got the attention it deserved. This habit continued well into his early teens, right up to his last visit to our house.

Khushil was a Brahmin by birth. Brahmin is a cast in Hinduism, and often associated with priests, teachers and protectors of the sacred hymns and prayers. One similar trait is found among the old Brahmin cult – they all have a sweet tooth. They are fond of Indian sweet delocalises such as 'ladoo' (ball shaped sweet made from flour and sugar) & 'puran rotli' (stuffed chapatti with sweet filling). Khushil was a true son of Brahmin, and was no different when it came to being fond of sweets. He would often request that Namrata visited our house, in the hopes of quenching his craving for ladoos. Namrata would sometimes call in advance, so that we could prepare the dish.

Almost all children have a favourite cuddly toy when they are growing up. For most people, this is a teddy bear, or a cuddly animal of some kind. For Khushil, this was simply a piece of cotton pink coloured cloth. This pink cloth was called 'Ouh'.

One day Khushil had accompanied my parents to the local high street. They went to the grocery shop and drove straight home. On arrival back at the house, Khushil noticed that his 'Ouh' was lost. The usually quiet boy spoke out. He demanded to have his 'Ouh' back. For a moment Khushil was a child again. It was pleasing to see him speak up, although less so to see his tears. He was so upset that my mum called the grocery store, who confirmed that the pink cloth had been left at the till. Luckily, the shop kept 'Ouh' aside and my mum rushed over to fetch it. When she returned his pink cloth back to him, he was thrilled. To date, my mum still says that this was the happiest she ever saw Khushil.

In July 2017, the Pandyas were carrying out some renovation work. They decided to come over to my house sister's house, to get ready for the day. Khushil was well known for being a perfectionist, and this applied to how he groomed himself. He liked to look after himself, with minimal help. Although he was in a frail condition at that point, and could barely stand, he bathed him himself, and then came downstairs and said, 'Priya, Didi, your house is well decorated but I could not find any mirrors in the bedroom to do my hair. Can you please put the camera on your phone so I can do this?' Khushil's standards were high, and he made sure that he kept to them.

Khushil's friends and family, including the teachers at Claremont High School, can testify to how disciplined this boy was. He touched so many lives through his short journey, and taught us all through his punctuality and discipline about what a 14-year-old boy really could achieve. His braveness in the face of such adversity is to be admired, all whilst keeping *that* smile on his face.

To this day, we remember and cherish the wonderful memories that we had with Khushil, and hold them close to our heart. Hopefully, one day, we will see another little Pandya enter the world. Keeping our fingers firmly crossed!

Yahtnavan (Khushil's Best Friend)

Khushil Pandya

First things first, 2008, I was a lonely kid but that was ok I was satisfied with watching the other kids play, one day 5-year-old me was minding my own business (being lonely) when a boy popped his head out of hiding from behind the climbing frames, "CAN YOU CATCH ME!", "BET YOU CAN'T CATCH ME!" … I had no idea what I was supposed to do I didn't even know this kid, so I just played along and chased the boy, in and out of the bushes until eventually I found him laying out of breath on a bench, I got him...

"Hi!" ... He screamed, even though I was right next to him... "I'm KOOSEL!!", and just like that, the first and easily the best friend I'll ever have in my life just popped into my life as easy as popping out from behind a climbing frame. Turns out he didn't have any friends either, so I was his first friend too, he made making friends look so easy...

Fast forward to year 3, it was just Khushil and me running through the lush forest of roe green... I brought my book of animals to see if we could find any insects in the bushes that matched the ones in the pictures in the book, Khushil taught me all creatures are beautiful, I'm still kind off disgusted by spiders and their appearance however I also know they deserve to wander the gardens on their own accord as much as I did. Respect to nature is key, and don't forget... a 7-year-old taught me this...

On to the next year, year 4 was one of the most influential years of my life because once again due to my inability to make friends... Khushil did karate and would always have debates with Kokul (who did taekwondo) as to which style is better, that's how I met Kokul, through Khushil... Nouh and Sanjay were friends with Kokul, that's how I met Nouh and Sanjay... Kailan, Khushil and I had origami and art competitions at breaktimes and that's how I met them... Miss Safi was our teacher and we were her first ever class so I guess our teacher added even more to the bonds that Khushil had created since we were all her favorite students...

I remember going over to Khushil's and being given offers of all sorts of delicious food by Khushil and his parents. I was scared I would eat their entire fridge and cupboards, Khushil's generosity was unparalleled. We would play Batman: Arkham City and try and take turns to beat up the bad guys in the most unthinkably creative ways possible! I guess that was my idea… maybe I'm a bad influence…

He taught me some karate kicks and his graffiti style art and teamed up with Sanjay to joke around about me liking a girl in our class, but it was all fun and games in the end…

For some reason, going into high school from year 6 separated me and Khushil, we still went to see each other but that happened less and less until 4 years went by and I was 14, he was 15, I did get Birthday messages and I sent them in return but that was about it, nevertheless I still considered him my best friend. Khushil made new friends and I made new friends whilst keeping old, I'm not sure if any friends from primary went to the same high school as Khushil however I was certain he was happy.

I started playing basketball seriously along with Kokul and Nouh and I met Dhanish and Sahil who also played basketball. I was still good friends with Sanjay and Kailan, turns out Dhanish and Sahil went to Khushil's tuition, and suddenly Dhanish tells me Khushil has passed away, I thought he was telling me a bad joke at first, I was silent for the day. No one knows this, but I was crying myself to sleep that day and days after not because I missed him (which I did) …

I cried because I did not get to say goodbye, I don't even remember the last thing I said to him, I had lost connection. I went to the funeral on a Saturday, from the speeches people were giving, especially the ones from Khushil's classmates, they all claimed him as their best friend...

For a minute jealousy filled my soul. But then I realized it was my own fault, I had been too heavy of a weight for the tightrope between us to hold together, I made it break, I caused myself to fall. If I had at least visited Khushil more this would never had happened. There are too many more stories I have about Khushil for this small piece of text but for those who are curious you'll need to ask me in person.

Even in leaving us Khushil taught me one last lesson... Never take people, love and happiness for granted, it can be taken away as fast as you receive it if you don't show gratitude for it in one way or another.

To this day I play basketball with shoes which have K.P. written on them to give me strength mentally and physically, to give me reason... I am only 5'6" which is short for basketball, yet I have become one of the top 3 players in my year group and I'm always getting better. However, I will never let anything, even basketball... destroy the bonds I have with the world and people around me...

I will forever be happy, I will be grateful, I will cherish the love I receive, I won't stop believing.

Thank you Khushil.

Dele Johnson (Friend)

My first encounter with Khushil was at the school office. I was studying mathematical equations, and I was stuck on a question, but I was just too embarrassed to ask anyone for help. Eventually I asked a colleague, who happened to be standing next to a small boy dressed in school uniform. The boy had short black hair, and he was clearly very shy. After explaining my dilemma to my colleague, he turned to the little boy and said, 'Khushil can help you.' I looked at Khushil and thought to myself, 'Surely this child cannot help me. He is only about 10 years old!' To my amazement, Khushil was able to calculate the correct answer, as well as explaining to me how he did it. I thanked him, and he smiled, before walking off casually as it was no big deal at all. Even at that age, Khushil was a selfless human being, who cared so much for others.

Over the years, Khushil and I built up a great relationship. There were times when he would get really excited updating me on his life adventures. He would get so excited that he almost always ended up stuttering out his words in the process. This was Khushil, 'Dele, come and check out my new drawings', 'Look at what I can do', as he pulled out his deck of magic cards or performed tricks on his Segway.

Khushil challenged my concept of life, by just being himself. Whether it was his persistent work ethic, or his organisation skills, he always made you think that you could do more with yourself, and that it's never too late to follow your dreams.

I will miss your physical presence, Khushil, but you are in my heart forever. You have left a legacy behind, in every person that you inspired.

Ms Claire El-Arifi (was Ms Butcher)

Year S class Teacher (Roe Green Junior School)

Teaching Khushil was always a pleasure. He was such a kind and gentle member of the class, who had many friends.

I will always remember at the end of the year, when the children brought in gifts for staff – Khushil had bought me a beautiful set of watercolour pencils. As a great lover of drawing, I remember feeling so touched by his thoughtful gift. I still have the pencils, and I always think of him when I use them.

Mr Cooke (Khushil's Maths Teacher Year 5)

(Roe Green Junior School)

Khushil had a real sense of justice, knowing what was right and what was wrong. He was not afraid to stand up to other children when he thought they were in the wrong.

Miss Safi (Khushil's Year 4 class teacher)

(Roe Green Junior School)

Khushil was a very quiet, caring and thoughtful young man, who looked after his friends and put a smile on their face.

Jalpa Pandya

Swami Shri:- "Spirited Soul"

One evening in March 2015, as I was leaving work, I received a phone call from Namrata. She told me that Khushil was in hospital, and had been diagnosed with a brain tumour. Immediately, I was overwhelmed with thoughts for this brave little soul, who was not aware of the tragedy unfolding. At first, I struggled to comprehend the news. I couldn't convince myself that life could change so quickly. I rushed to the hospital, picking up my son Hem, Khushil's friend from school, on the way.

This was the first time in my working life that I had taken leave for the Easter break, to stay for Khushil for his hospital visits. I remember being there when they said he had 6 months to live. We walked home that day with Khushil, feeling shaken to the core. Luckily, he didn't know about the diagnosis, and somehow I think that this helped me to stand on my own two feet and be strong for him.

During the treatment, much to his dismay, his physical appearance changed an awful lot. Despite this, I always found him to be calm, patient, tolerant and hopeful that this would soon pass. Later I realised that this was in fact all an act. He had googled every word that had been said to him by the doctors. He knew his diagnosis, and what his circumstances were. But despite all of that, he wanted us to feel better. He was utterly selfless.

Whilst going through this new and difficult stage of life with Khushil, I witnessed him taking extra care to maintain his routine as much as possible. He attended school regularly, worked towards achieving good grades, and spent time with friends. He improved his art and piano skills, whilst still working hard at table tennis, and started taekwondo. This all seems unbelievable, but he had a remarkable spirit.

Even during challenging times, when his body wouldn't follow his brain's instructions, he still wore the mask of a smile. He still tried to communicate, using his remarkable invention – just another one of his contributions to this world. When asked ,'Hi Khushil, Kem Che?' (How are you?) there was always one response, "Maja"(Fine). This continued even until his final day. Khushil defied all medical expectations, Khushil had a special relationship with me and Hem. Remembering him saying, 'Jalpa aunty ave che?' (Is Jalpaaunty coming?), or 'Hem avec he?' (Is Hem coming?) still kills me. I still look forward to seeing him walking through the front gates, to and from his school. In the last few days of his physical existence, I still remember him enthusiastically asking Namrata to serve Hem orange jelly, even though he himself was dependant on water dripping through his nose for survival.

It was a privilege for me and Hem to be present when

such a spirited soul departed, but he is still with us, and always will be, accepting challenges and sailing through them.

A special message for Khushil from Hem: 'I Miss You.'

Mr Riggs (Khushil's Head of Year)

It was my great privilege to have been Khushil's Head of Year for the 3 years in which he attended Claremont High School. I can say, without a shadow of a doubt, that no other student has had a bigger impact on me as a teacher and a human being. He was, and remains, an inspiration to all that had the pleasure of being part of Khushil's life.

Khushil was not loud, and did not seek the limelight. He did not make crowd rousing speeches or deliver breathtaking performances at the school shows. Khushil inspired through the quiet, methodical, determination that he exhibited every day of his life. He inspired through his attention to detail, his wit, his stubborn will to improve and succeed, his love of science, music, football, art and the natural world. Never have I known a student with more passion, dedication and commitment to his studies. He loved school, and those that taught him were awe struck by the positive attitude that he showed towards his learning.

Of course, what made Khushil's achievements even more astounding was the fact they were achieved against a backdrop of such cruel adversity. Khushil ensured all his medical appointments and treatment would take place before or after school. In the final months, as his physical mobility deteriorated, the perseverance shown to simply get to school was astonishing, to go on to achieve so much even more so. Khushil did not see his illness as something that would stop him. It was just another life hurdle that could be overcome – as always with dignity and tenacity.

One of Khushil's proudest achievements was the completion of the Duke of Edinburgh Award. Many people, myself included, questioned whether this would be possible. As usual, this stubborn and determined young man ignored us and achieved what he set out to achieve. That was Khushil, the very definition of mind over matter. If I could bottle his passion, attitude and spirit, I would. I'd give it to every student that passed through the school gates, not to mention my son, every day of his life.

On Khushil's final day at school, in July 2017, he received the award for Boy of the Year. As he accepted the award, the entire hall rose up to give a standing ovation in honour of his achievements. It was a moment to savour, and a reminder that you do not have to shout to be heard. His quiet, stubborn determination had raised the roof.

It makes me incredibly sad to think of Khushil's passing, but at the same time amazingly proud and thankful that I was able to witness some of his many accomplishments. Khushil burnt bright in his short life, and will continue to inspire me and others as we move forward.

A true inspiration.

Ms Arbani (Science Teacher – Claremont High School)

The wonderful scientific learner: Khushil

Khushil inspired others through his love of learning, and especially through his love of science. He was always willing to make his contribution during science lessons and never failed to impress me as a teacher. This young man had a thirst for knowledge and he knew that school was where his thirst would be quenched.

After completing the topic of forces and motion, Khushil designed the most amazing revision poster, which incorporated all the things he had learnt. His understanding of Physics was brilliant, in particular his layout of calculations using equations of motion. His diagrams were beautifully illustrated, for example when he was explaining circular motion he drew the London Eye, which he used to focus upon Newton's second Law of motion, $F = ma$ and how it should be used for exam questions.

His poster was an artistic resource, which I have kept to show other pupils. When other pupils view his work, they understand just how much he loved science. The length of time he took, making sure every piece of work was of the highest possible standard, was inspirational.

Khushil's science exercise book was a joy to behold. He took every care to make sure that his classwork and homework were completed with precision and pride. His book will always be talked about, as he was a model pupil, who understood the merits of what a good education can provide. He valued every aspect of the content he was being taught and knew the answers to every question he was asked.

Teaching Khushil in year 8 and year 9 was a true privilege. It is very rare to come across such a polite, respectful and wonderful young man who was genuinely honest and humble.

Khushil will always be my point of reference, as an example of an excellence whenever I want to encourage other pupils to do well. We will continue to celebrate his life at Claremont, using his work as an example of what others can achieve.

Khushil, you were a wonderful smiling scientific learner, who graced my classroom. Thank you for bringing us so much joy! Your star will go on shining, forever and ever.

Your thankful teacher, Ms Arbani

Dr. Mari Chikvaidze (Maths Teacher – Claremont High School)

My Khushil,

I remember noticing a rather shy student in a class of loud and hyperactive year 9s, during my first week at Claremont. Khushil was one of the first students whose kind and gentle eyes made me feel welcome.

Khushil was very popular in class. Even the most difficult kids would change their behaviour completely when seated next to him. He had this magical power of making everything and everyone around him a tiny bit better. Khushil's constant attention to everything discussed in class, his diligence with homework, and his insatiable thirst for making progress in Maths, was contagious indeed. I remember at one point, when he could no longer write, there was a competition for who would scribe for him. He had an extraordinary influence. People, including myself, were drawn towards him because of his ability to bring out the best of our qualities, both personal and academic. When Khushil's health started to deteriorate, this magical ability of his got even stronger. He would keep on coming to school, doing the work, and asking for extension sheets. He kept on completing the homework. Despite his energy levels being low, his spirits were high, and his drive to succeed was stronger than ever. And as time went on, Khushil managed to completely transform a class that I had initially dreaded teaching. Because of Khushil, I walked into that class with a huge smile on my face. Every lesson became a fairy tale, where our classroom was enchanted by kindness, compassion and love.

Towards the end, it was all about Khushil for us. He loved his school, he loved his teachers, he loved his friends, and we all loved him back – with a kind of never ending love that's very hard to express in words. Khushil's picture is still in our classroom, and we still have our Maths lessons in just the way he liked them. He is the driving force behind everything we do. Khushil's friends continue following his example, and keep spirits high, even when things go wrong. It is Khushil who gives us strength and motivation to love what we do, and to do our best to get better at it.

I feel blessed to have been able to spend a few precious months in the same classroom with Khushil. I witnessed something remarkable, in this shy and humble year 9 boy. My time with Khushil touched me deeply. I miss Khushil, like many of us do, but I am also grateful to him, for inspiring me to be the best teacher I can be, and for making such a profound impact on his friends in year 10, and everyone else who knew him at Claremont.

Ms E McGuinness (Khushil's Class Teacher – Claremont High School)

Khushil will forever have a lasting place in my memories. His positivity towards life was contagious. Each time he entered his form class or science class he brought with him a love for learning. Khushil was strong minded, funny, and determined to achieve his best in everything he did.

Every now and again I look down at the back of my form class, and remember his presence. Although Khushil is not there in person, I know he is watching over his form and smiling.

Ms C Taylor (Deputy Head of Year 9 – Claremont High School)

Khushil was always someone special in our year group. Right from year 7, he made an impact with his fun-loving attitude and strong-minded ways. Khushil made some fantastic friends in his form group, where his memory will forever live on. I would describe Khushil as someone who was driven and determined to get what they want. Additionally, he was a very hardworking student, who loved coming to school. Khushil is an inspiration to us all, in the way that he demonstrated resilience and overcame adversity. He is, and will always be, greatly missed.

Ms Perkins (English Teacher) (Claremont High School)

In September 2016 a polite young man walked into my room, apologised for being early for the lesson, and asked if he could come in and read before the lesson started. A few minutes later we started discussing the book that he was reading. I was surprised that a year 9 boy knew so much about the author and other works published by him.

This was the first time I met Khushil. From that moment onwards, he impressed me with his wider knowledge of the topics we studied. He had an extraordinary love for learning, and would always go the extra mile to research or read about the topics we were studying. Khushil was always well organised, well equipped, and well ahead of the others.

Khushil stood out with his ability to write in an entertaining style, and his ability to work independently or in a group, but most of all he stood out for his ability to speak to an audience. During presentations he would engage the audience with his wit, knowledge and power to persuade. Following our final class presentation, Khushil was voted the best speaker, and received a standing ovation when he finished. Khushil was very modest and popular with his peers. Pupils liked being in his group because he worked diligently and made them all look good.

As the summer approached, Khushil came up to the third floor of the English block on crutches for his lesson. When I told him that we would relocate to a room on the ground floor, he just smiled. He said, 'You don't have to do that.' Soon, Khushil was travelling around the school in his wheelchair. His classmates became very protective of him, and made sure that there was always a fence of pupils around him. This was a testament to the kind of friend Khushil was.

The standard of Khushil's work never deteriorated. His homework and classwork were always of a very high standard. His writing was often used as an example for others. He was highly motivated in English, and whatever the topic was he contributed enthusiastically, and wrote about it exceptionally well.

Eventually, Khushil began to use his phone to type his responses; the quality remained outstanding. Khushil would not let anything get in the way of success. He firmly believed in attending every lesson and did his absolute best from the moment the lesson began. The one English lesson he missed, I was emailed by his mum requesting the work, and the next day he arrived with it completed and ahead of the class as usual. I have never witnessed any young person as determined as Khushil. He was an exceptional pupil and an outstanding personality. He will always be remembered, and our memories of him will live on. Khushil was friendly, firm and fearless.

On a personal note, I will remember Khushil as one of the most knowledgeable, dedicated, enthusiastic, outstanding pupils I have ever taught. Khushil was truly exceptional.

Ms Bhavan Patel (Khushil's Geography Teacher – Claremont High School)

When I first met Khushil, I saw just a normal little boy. In many ways, he was just that, however in other ways I completely underestimated him. Khushil Pandya was the most inspiring, motivated and ambitious pupils that I have ever had the pleasure of teaching. I feel privileged to have had the opportunity to teach him, and I cannot help but smile when I think of him.

I still remember the day when I first met Khushil. He was so small, that I asked him to sit at the front of the class, because otherwise he wouldn't have been able to see the board! The look he gave me when I said this…suddenly I realised that within this small, very sweet looking package was a huge personality, and that Khushil was not someone to underestimate. From that point on, my admiration for him grew immeasurably, and continued to grow with every passing lesson.

I can honestly say that I have never met anybody with the energy and drive that Khushil showed, not only for his studies, but for life. His hunger to learn was second to none. His desire to live on his own terms blew me away. Khushil would accept nothing less than the best. Getting 98% on a test, being specially selected to go on a reward trip, and even being voted student of the year, wasn't enough for Khushil. He was always trying to improve, to better himself. This doesn't mean he didn't know how to have a bit of fun though. He would throw a smile every time he knew that he had said something cheeky, and pushed the boundaries a little.

The strange thing is, I think Khushil taught me more than I could ever teach him. I learnt so much from this little man about what it means to live life to the fullest, and to aspire to be the best in all that you do. He has made me a better teacher. Now, every time I meet new students, I don't assume that they are just a normal little boy or girl, because I realise I could be so wrong.

Every time I think of Khushil, I feel richer for having met him. Thank you, Khushil.

Mr Page (Claremont High School)

I first met Khushil when he came to Learning Support one afternoon, to borrow one of the iPads we had. He wanted to use it in his lessons, to type up his notes. In many ways, Khushil borrowing an iPad to take notes on, sums up his attitude to learning. If you put a problem in front of him then he would simply find a way to overcome to it. Even as things became more difficult for Khushil, he *always* found new ways of getting on with his studies, and achieving his goals. Nothing was going to stand in his way.

As the summer months progressed, we saw more of Khushil in Learning Support for one reason or another, and we were very fortunate to be able to get know him a little, and to be able to provide some assistance. He was truly an inspirational young person. I never heard him complain or grumble about anything. He continued to score top marks in assessments, he always came to school, he kept a fine sense of humour, and he was always polite. He was always a lovely, gentle young person to be around.

Even when things became difficult for Khushil, it felt like, in a way, he made the school a better place to be in. He brought out, or highlighted, the best in people, from his classmates to the wider pupil population and the staff team. People were keen to help out where they could, because it was for Khushil – because he was so well liked and so highly thought of.

I miss Khushil, and am very sorry that he is no longer with us, but I have very fond and special memories of him. He achieved so much, and what a fine example he set in doing so. He won't be forgotten.

Ms Varshita Vella (Shah – Claremont High School)

When I was first asked to write a message in memorandum of Khushil, I sat and stared for a while. I was apprehensive about writing something about Khushil, out of fear that I wouldn't be able to do him justice. Then I thought, 'What would Khushil say to me, if he were here right now?' He certainly would have not settled for any apprehension or doubt. Instead, he would have given me reassurance and confidence to face my fears. This, in my opinion, sums up Khushil for me. Selfless, bold and fearless. Always.

During year 9, Khushil spent an increasing amount of time working in the Hub, due to his health becoming more challenging. I was concerned that he may feel intimidated by the older Year 10 and 11 students who also frequented the Hub, but in fact it was quite the opposite. Khushil spoke with confidence to the other students, some of whom have incredibly big personalities, and soon became somewhat of a celebrity of the Hub. Students of all ages would cheer as he came in, older students would turn to him for advice, and take heed of his words far more than my own. When he wasn't there, students would miss him and ask after him.

Khushil was invaluable from the very first day, and it was incredible to watch his positive energy ripple through the school. He had an influence that none of us could ever have imagined. When in his company, students and teachers would leave feeling pumped and invigorated, whether it was from his positivity, or his wicked sense of humour.

Headstrong is a word used to describe him by many people; when Khushil had his mind set on something, he would not stop until he achieved it. He helped many people, but I'd say my most personal memory of him was during one lunchtime, just before the May half term. He came into the Hub for lunch, and saw a couple of students filling sweetie bags for my wedding. He asked if I needed any help, to which of course I happily said yes. He offered to help fill the bags, but it was quite a fiddly job. I offered something else for him to do, but he was determined to fill the bags with sweets. Towards the end, he struggled, and so he said he would take a break from filling, and offer words of support to the rest of us to help us finish quickly. He did exactly that, and made us laugh along the way. We finished and the students left, and he stayed behind, gave me a beaming smile and whispered to me, 'I can't come to your wedding, so when you eat the sweets on your wedding day, you can think of me! I'm glad I get to be a part of it!' It was one of the most heartfelt things anyone has ever done or said to me. Sure enough, when I saw all my guests eating the sweets on my wedding day, I thought of him!

Khushil had no idea how much his joy spread, and how much light he could bring to people's lives, even in the darkest of moments. He never expected anything in return, just the opportunity to do what he wanted to do. He inspired so many of us, students and teachers alike. His legacy continues; challenged students continue to take his advice, as do those who were brought together by Khushil, and those who he motivated and inspired. Khushil is alive in each person whose heart he touched, and by telling his story, he will live on.

Ms Carswell (Duke Of Edinburgh Manager – Claremont High School)

I met Khushil for the first time when he signed up to do the Duke of Edinburgh (DofE) Bronze Award, in November

2016. That year was the first year that Claremont has run DofE Awards as a fully licensed organisation, since the 1980s.

I quickly realised that Khushil was no ordinary 13-year-old boy. He demonstrated an abundance of enthusiasm in all of the DofE afterschool sessions. Khushil chose piano for the skill section of the award, and Taekwondo for his physical section. He didn't waste any time in clocking up the required hours in both activities, and was one of the quickest in the year group to complete one whole section – Taekwondo – which he did for three months, finishing on 1st February 2017! Khushil decided to develop his piano performance for the longer term of six months. He completed it on 20th April 2017. Both very impressive achievements.

With his decreasing mobility, in April 2017, Khushil's doctors suggested that he should not take part in the expedition section. With this advice, Mrs Pandya and I had a conversation about particular afterschool expedition preparation sessions. It was suggested that Khushil wouldn't take part in certain sections, so that he wouldn't become disheartened. When I started asking Khushil a few days later about what sessions he wanted to do, he quickly interrupted me, and said, 'ALL of them!' It soon became clear that he was more than determined to take part in any expeditions that he could, and after many talks between the doctors, Mrs Pandya, Khushil, myself and the DofE London head office, we came up with a plan – enabling Khushil to take part in every single bit of his expedition section, and pass it with flying colours.

As Khushil demonstrated such passion towards his own DofE Award, an obvious option for his volunteering section was to help the delivery and promotion of the programme at Claremont. He helped me to ensure that the expedition would be feasible to complete with a wheelchair, through a number of conversations. He also made a wonderful poster and provided an inspirational quote to help promote DofE Awards to future participants. These are now displayed on our DofE central notice board, along with Khushil's quote: "DofE increased my self-confidence and made me new friends who I trust with all my heart. It was an unforgettable experience. I wish everyone would take up this once in a lifetime opportunity!"

All 27 students passed the expedition. 14, Khushil included, completed their other 3 sections in time to receive their full Bronze Award certificates in a presentation assembly, on Wednesday 12th July 2017. Certificates and badges were presented to them by special guests Barry Gardiner, Labour MP for Brent North and Jo Amand, Operations Manager at DofE London.

The DofE promotion was proven to be very successful, as the award uptake expanded from a total of 27 pupils in year one, to a total of 89 pupils in year 2. I believe that Khushil was a significant influence on this huge increase. 23 of the 27 in Khushil's cohort continued from the Bronze Award to the Silver, and an additional 22 in his year group signed up for the Silver Award as direct entrants, having been inspired by the humble young man who completed all four sections of his DofE

Award before many others. Khushil was one of the first pupils to achieve their full DofE Award delivered through Claremont in over 30 years!

On November 14th 2017, we held our DofE celebration evening, where a further 6 pupils were able to collect their full award along with the original 14. Mrs Pandya came up on Khushil's behalf, along with the other participants, to receive a huge round of applause for their achievement. A number of awards were given out during the evening, including best team worker and most organised. The last award was titled 'Most Inspirational'. I felt so privileged to present the award to Khushil's parents on his behalf, and deliver my speech detailing the young man who broke barriers and defied all odds.

I was so honoured to be present during the celebration of Khushil's life on Saturday 9th September. The courage demonstrated by Mr and Mrs Pandya throughout the day filled everyone with pure admiration. Over the next few days, I was surprised to find that I was not consumed by the overwhelming amounts of sadness that I expected. Instead, I felt an extraordinary strength, ever present within and all around me, which I know was Khushil. Although I was sorrowful from loss, this presence comforted me, as I knew he was there with us all.

Above my desk on my notice board, I have a very special photo. In this photo, Khushil and his expedition team are pictured looking ecstatic, having just been told by the DofE assessors that they had passed their qualifying expedition. Their group was the first group to finish, which was a massive achievement. This photo gives me great strength whenever I look at it. Now, if I feel at all demotivated at work, I look at this photo and say 'Sorry Khushil!', as I am immediately reminded that everything will be brighter and more positive, just as long as I continue my day with the same enthusiasm and zest for life that Khushil showed, each and every single moment. Khushil received the 'Most Inspirational' award at the DofE celebration evening. However, he was not only inspirational as a DofE participant – he was the most inspirational person I have ever met!

Dr Dusza (Duke of Edinburgh-Claremont High School)

My amazing story with Khushil started with the Duke of Edinburgh Bronze Award, in November 2016. I had seen Khushil many times around school, but I wasn't lucky enough to have ever taught him. I know that Khushil loved Science, and had very good understanding of it. He was absolutely passionate about Biology, especially animals. I remember once, during the expedition packing session, we started talking about food and the reason why it should be well protected. I was talking about bacteria, when Khushil interrupted me, and said 'Yes, but what about mammals?' I asked him what he meant, and he said, 'The food has to be protected from bears, wolves, and foxes.' I assured him that except maybe some foxes we shouldn't be bothered by the other animals. He nodded and added, 'But still it has to be protected from them. Maybe not here, but in some parks, there are bears.' 'Have you ever seen any

222

bears?' I asked with noticeable doubt in my voice. 'Yes, with my parents when we went to America.' Khushil travelled a lot with his parents, but would only share the stories which involved some aspect of biology. It looked like nothing else could be more interesting for him. I tried to talk to him at times about Physics, since I know some interesting facts about the subject, but each time he would finish these discussions quickly. One such example was on the day when we were preparing for the expedition. Khushil and I were checking his rucksack, and at certain points we started talking about his trips with his parents. When he mentioned the Northern Lights, I stopped from excitement and asked, 'It must be amazing to experience it, right?' He looked at me blankly, and after two or three seconds, he said, 'Shall we carry on packing?' It was one of the first times, and not the last one, when I learnt that the last word belonged to Khushil. I tried one more time to talk about these lights, and received nothing in return. Instead, I was told a story about large birds of prey, hawks, and eagles indicating his real interest and love for animals.

He always loved to share his opinion with others, and if he disagreed then he made sure they knew in the best possible way. Khushil was slowly but gradually losing his mobility and vision, but certainly not the sharpness of his brain. On the first day of the practice expedition, it was a hot day, above 25 degrees, and we had already been walking for a couple of hours. The group was tired, but had a positive spirit. After a longer break, the students took the maps, gave one to Khushil and started to discuss the direction they should carry on walking, without consulting Khushil. They walked maybe two minutes, when Khushil asked one of his team members to stop pushing the wheelchair. Soon, the group realised that Khushil was not following them, turned back and asked for the reason. Without arguing, he calmly announced, 'You're walking the wrong way. I am not following you.' They checked the map again, including him this time, and realised that he was right. All of us learned fast that Khushil was very good at navigation, and the group ensured they always discussed further actions with him. Not being a great navigator myself, I was extremely impressed with him. Khushil knew his strengths and weaknesses, and would never deny them. If he could do something by himself, he would try to the bitter end. When he needed help, on the other hand, he would ask and allow us to do it for him. His faith in his own knowledge and logic was truly admirable.

During the qualifying expedition, after almost eight hours of walking, we were all exhausted, sweaty and hungry. We were told that behind the field in front of us was a nice path that would bring us directly to the campsite. We were walking and walking, and it looked like we would never reach this point. The sun was gone, dusk had come, but we were still walking in this long, stony and uneven field. The wheelchair was getting bogged down what seemed like every five seconds. Everyone was exhausted, but Khushil always looked happy. At some point we decided that we would carry the wheelchair. We grabbed the wheelchair in three and were carrying it along the uneven terrain. I do not remember being so exhausted in my life. I periodically checked on Khushil, to check if everything was fine, and he was still smiling. We covered about 200 metres, but it felt like two kilometres. We were so happy that we made it that we almost ran to the campsite. After dinner I approached Khushil. We started talking about the best and worst parts of the day, his mood and feelings. He said, 'Walking was the best part of the expedition because I could move and watch the animals, observe nature, see the birds and trees.' Then I added jokily (as I had developed a great relationship with him!), 'Well, it might be because you didn't have to wear a heavy rucksack and you had someone push you the whole time.' He added, 'Yes, but they enjoyed it too and the one who pushed me did not have to carry a rucksack. I am happy because we made it!' It is true that he did not have to walk all this time, however, his wheelchair was not adapted to the paths in the forest or the fields we had to cross. I saw him being jolted around in the wheelchair a lot of the time. Nevertheless, he never complained that he was uncomfortable or that he felt any pain. This is how he was, positive and ready to absorb everything from his surroundings. If only I could get a bit more from him about the Northern lights...!

Dr Shankar (Khushil's Consultant at UCLH)

Khushil Pandya: What can I say? A redoubtable young man. My abiding memory of him will be of his indomitable spirit, that gave him the strength to battle the advancing disease ravaging his body, and his never-say-die attitude of "Let's get on with life". He lived life to the full, never wasting a nanosecond. Never will I meet a more courageous boy, with invincible determination.

While he appeared slightly built with an easy and winning manner, appearances cannot be more deceptive! His baby face belied his inner strength and mental toughness. In fact, as a budding taekwondo martial artist he embodied the taekwondo spirit of courtesy, loyalty, commitment, and respect to all. He would always demand a late OP appointment, so as to not miss a single day of class during his crippling illness! His perfect school attendance award is an example to all children.

His prized gold "Mont Blanc" ball pen was his treasure, and I believe I am the only person other than him to be privileged to have held and wrote with it! Not even his parents were allowed to use it

The "Khushil reading chart" speaks volumes for his ingenuity - this was a paper chart that he designed, with letters in colour coded boxes for communication when he lost the power of speech.

He fulfilled every obligation and commitment he undertook, and his word was his bond, and everyone knew it. I never heard him utter a word in anger or defeat.

What he has achieved in his short life, most of us will not achieve in our life time, and he reminds me very much of a quote by Erika Harris, "*I'm less interested in why we're here. I'm wholly devoted to while we're here*".

Dr R Sayed (Our GP)

I was never allowed to think of Khushil as a patient. Khushil never allowed this.

He was always a truly inspiring child. Stoical and determined to live life to the full.

When Khushil came to see me at the surgery for routine appointments, I always felt as if he was the carer, accompanying his mother. He was always so strong and never complained of any ailments.

I really looked forward to seeing Khushil, as he was leading such an exciting life! Our consultation time would always overrun, as he would fill me in on all the wild and wonderful things he had been up to since we last met – all beautifully captured on his mother's phone. I often commented to his parents that, had it not been for Khushil, they would not have experienced the riches of this world. Khushil's passion for learning and nature took him and his family to all the corners of the globe.

Despite being given a terminal prognosis, Khushil strived for only the best – living each day to the fullest and making it count. He left a trail of memories behind him, remaining positive throughout. I was always touched by the complete disregard that he had for his own health, only worrying about whether his mother was eating and looking after herself. Such admirable traits in one so young.

He did have a cheeky side also. He took much pleasure in seeing his mum squirm when she had to have her annual flu jab. Khushil would be close by, giving support, with a little smile on his face!

I was privileged to look after Khushil through his final journey. As his condition deteriorated and he lost his ability to walk and then speak, he remained determined to continue to make the most of the time he had left. He never wanted his illness to define him, and it never did.

Khushil will be remembered for all his achievements and accolades, and for what he gave to all those around him. He truly touched the lives of those he encountered.

His strength and courage will always be an example to others.

Catherine Aldridge (Children's Community Nurse)

Khushil was one of those young men that you very rarely meet. He had a strength and an understanding of himself, to an extent that was very unusual of someone of his age, and an incredible sense of self-discipline. Khushil had many talents, as well as an excellent academic record. Academia was highly important to him, so whenever he made an appointment with us, he would try to do it outside of school days.

In the last part of his life, Khushil defied the expectations of most of us, and to his enormous credit was able to complete his Duke of Edinburgh Award. This was typical Khushil. He refused to be limited by the seriousness of his illness. He wanted to carry on with his life, and live it well, to the utmost of his ability. And so, he did.

I will always remember Khushil's determination,

knowledge and wisdom beyond his years, but most of all I will remember his wry smile, that he would so often give.

Tanya Boggs (UCLH Palliative of Care)

Khushil was truly exceptional! Writing this, I find it difficult to believe that I only knew him for 6 months.

I met this brave and determined young man for the first time in March 2017, when there was some concern that his tumour had progressed again. As far as Khushil was concerned, he had only temporarily stopped taekwondo because he wanted a rest. His love for his parents was evident in his wish at all times to protect them from his illness, and the associated worry.

As I got to know Khushil, I would respond to his questions with honesty and compassion, and be led by his mature and questioning nature. In the early days this meant that Khushil set me homework – and it wasn't easy! This I think was his way of testing my honesty and integrity. Once this had been established, he started asking more direct questions relating to his health. On one such occasion I know his dad really didn't want me to answer Khushil's question, which related to his changing physical condition. However, I could see the challenge in Khushil's eyes, and I knew if I were anything less than honest our connection would be broken, and he would stop asking.

Khushil was highly intelligent, having a keen interest in science, investigating all sorts of health issues via the internet. He told me he had not searched for his diagnosis online, but had looked into certain changes in his condition as and when they occurred. He always listened respectfully to professional opinion and advice, and then took time to consider what it meant for him. He remained hopeful, and was always keen to understand why he couldn't have surgery or other treatments. I only once saw him tearful, when we were discussing treatment options, and he asked specifically about a cure. He understood the consequences of not having any treatment. At that point I apologised that I didn't have better news for him. It shouldn't have surprised me when Khushil told me that while he was angry at his situation, he wasn't angry with me or the other professionals involved in his care, and that I had nothing to apologise for. He then asked for confirmation that his parents knew the situation. Again, his focus was on his parents and their distress and sadness, as well as his friends and teachers at school, rather than himself.

When faced with a new challenge or problem, rather than feeling sorry for himself, Khushil always resolved to find a solution, and continue with living life to the fullest.

When his mobility was failing, Khushil remained hopeful by comparing himself to Professor Stephen Hawking. Just because his body didn't work, it didn't mean that his brain couldn't still achieve great things. This determination meant that he continued to attend school, and achieved his bronze Duke of Edinburgh award.

When he was losing the ability to speak, and I was suggesting potential apps, Khushil had in his mind a practical solution that he had seen on "The Theory of Everything". He worked with a speech therapist to develop this aid – which allowed him to continue to have his voice heard. Although no longer able to speak, Khushil still asked questions – they were typed into his phone and saved until I next visited. Although I no longer got given homework, I was challenged by his direct and probing questions, right up until the day before he died.

Helping Khushil and his parents through this desperately sad time was a privilege, and I am humbled that I was given the opportunity to meet such an inspiration. Khushil achieved so much in his 14 years, much more than those of us who have lived longer could ever hope to achieve.

Hayley Randall

My perception of Khushil:

I only had the pleasure of meeting him once, however I knew so much about him before that meeting. I first knew of him around 2 years prior, through working with him mum, Nam.

I still remember the day she called me to tell me she had to take him to the opticians, as his sight wasn't quite right, and how in the next few weeks everything seemed to spiral out of control.

What had started as a check-up at the optician (my perception) soon became many hospital appointments, with far more serious consequences.

Throughout those years I got to know a lot about Khushil.

He looked like an ordinary boy on the outside, however he had extraordinary values and kindness on the inside.

It blew me away how much effort he made to maintain a normal lifestyle – going to school, asking for homework, and planning for the next term. He loved school and reading, it was never in doubt that he could be anything he wanted to be.

Khushil had a real love for life, and made the absolute most of every opportunity that presented itself to him. Through his choice to explore Alaska, his love of football and meeting Sir Alex Ferguson and Sir Bobby Charlton, meeting Dynamo, not once but three times, and going to the tennis to watch Novak Djokovic and Roger Federer, he was making the most of each day.

Khushil had a huge heart, and his thoughts were always with others, even down to the smallest things – like sending Fererro Rocher into work with Nam, just to put a smile on my face.

The support he gave to Nam and Bhavesh without even realising it was beyond anything a parent could expect from their child. He was always asking why Nam wasn't at work, and always encouraging her to get to work and to push forward with her exams. He was the pillar that got them both through the tough days, and made things seem brighter.

On the day I met Khushil, I realised that everything I had heard about him was absolutely true. Standing in his room, surrounded by his things, seeing his school projects and his teddies, the books that he'd read and the stars on the ceiling and most importantly the smile on his face – even that day he managed to light up the room, and I knew I was talking to someone very special.

Khushil was an angel, who will always look down on us. Forever in our hearts and prayers.

Charlotte Howarth (Funeral Care- Co Op Funeral Services)

On the 5th September 2017, I was sat at my desk working my way through emails, and getting myself organised, when the phone rang. A gentleman was on the phone, asking me questions, and generally looking for information. It wasn't until I started to ask questions that I was introduced to Khushil. I was told a fourteen-year-old boy had passed away the previous evening. My heart sank. I said to the gentleman, 'Please call me if you need anything. Otherwise, I will be in touch soon.' From that moment on, Khushil was at the forefront of my mind.

When I arrived at Khushil's home, I sat in my car for a little while. I had an overwhelming feeling of nervousness. I am confident in my practice; I know my paperwork back to front. However, I was very aware that I was about to walk into someone's home, where their young son has just passed away. Their son had been taken away from them, and was now in our care. In that moment, I was reminded of the importance of reassuring these parents that we would care for their beloved son, and cast my nerves to one side.

Khushil's parents came into the branch to bring me his clothes and personal belongings. We sat on the sofa and went through his clothes, so I could write everything down. As Namrata, Khushil's mother, went through each item of clothing, I couldn't help but feel heartbroken for them. His clothes were so small, and typical of a young teenage boy. Namrata went through each item, explaining how Khushil would have worn these. I wanted to make sure I had a detailed description. This was something that was so important to Khushil and his parents, and I needed to ensure these wishes were carried out. One of Khushil's personal items was a sacred cord or upavita. It was important that the cord was to be placed over Khushil's left shoulder, across his chest and under his right arm, under his clothes. I remember the importance of this, and I think I went through it a few times with Namrata to make sure I had it right. It may sound simple enough, but these are the things that made Khushil, Khushil.

Some days passed, and I knew Khushil was due to rest in the chapel with me in our Kingsbury Branch. Anticipating his arrival, I set up the chapel of rest ready for his arrival. Andy and Darryl, two colleagues of mine arrived at the branch with Khushil, both providing the level of care one would expect when bringing someone's loved one to the chapel of rest. They both bought the coffin into the chapel, and as I stood to the side with my hands together, I hung my head at the little coffin being gently positioned. We opened the coffin and there he was. A lovely, handsome young man – dressed in his jeans, T-shirt, and plaid shirt with the top button undone. He also had a SpongeBob SquarePants teddy and white blanket by his side. I checked with Andy and Darryl that he had everything he was meant to, including two religious items, one of which had to be placed across his chest. I made sure this was the right way round, and positioned his blanket under his arm, sitting SpongeBob up at the end of the coffin.

I had arranged with Khushil's mum that they and some other family members would be coming in to visit with Khushil. From experience, I know what an emotional event the first visit can be. The coffin, the chapel…just being in the branch can be distressing. But when they arrived there was an air of calm. I slowly walked them to the chapel of rest. I explained the layout of the room and where Khushil was resting. I remember everyone taking off their shoes before they entered the room, which touched me. I knocked on the door and entered, moving to the side so everyone was able to come in. Namrata smiled at her son and stroked his forehead. I bit my lip to keep myself from crying, my heart broke for them all. I left the room and went to my office.

I wanted to make sure that Khushil's parents were aware that they could come and see their son whenever they wanted to; all they needed to do was let me know. These moments are so precious – they are the last moments with their son. They were entitled to spend these moments together as a family. As I sat Mr Bear on his seat, and tucked Khushil in with SpongeBob, the tears filled my eyes again. Every evening was the same.

I relied on my colleagues a lot during this time. As funeral directors, our own families don't understand the full extent of how emotionally draining our jobs can be.

So, we rely on each other for support. To say I work within an amazing, supportive, kind, and generous team would be an understatement. Everyone is always willing to bend over backwards for each other and our families. So much work goes into planning the funerals and talking to the families, as well as in the offices and out on funerals. I am very proud to be among such great people, and thank them for all the support they have shown.

Alison had been nominated to conduct Khushil's funeral. I was pleased, as Alison had helped me in the days coming up to the funeral, and she already knew a lot about Khushil. She called to do the pre-funeral call. We went through the details again, as we always do, ensuring all our information matched up. We were apprehensive about the day of the funeral. We all strive for perfection, and there is always a sense of sadness when the day of the funeral arrives – the final journey of a loved one, whom we have spent a lot of time with. There was a genuine feeling of sadness amongst us, whilst we worked with Khushil and his family. Listening to his family speak so highly of him, my colleagues expressing how handsome he was, and how lovely his eyelashes were – Khushil left a mark on us all.

Friday 8th September 2017 was my last day with Khushil. I was upset that he had to leave, and anxious to make sure that everything was in place for the day of the funeral, especially as I wasn't going to be in the branch to see him off. We went through our routine of moving SpongeBob, turning up the lights and the general morning chit chat. I told Namrata that I would be thinking of them tomorrow, and I hoped that they had a safe flight, as they had planned to take Khushil's ashes to India the following day.

The day had come to an end, and I had exhausted every excuse to stay. I went into the chapel to say my goodbyes to Khushil and tucked him up for the last time. I rested SpongeBob back under his arm, and told Khushil to keep him there. I pulled the vale over the coffin, and with teary eyes said goodbye. It was a pleasure to have met Khushil, despite wishing that I hadn't.

I often think about Khushil and his family, and how brave they all are. Khushil and his sheer determination, and love for life is inspiring. Six months after the funeral, Alison and I were approached by Namrata again, and it wasn't until this point that we found out how truly inspiring Khushil was. Speaking with Namrata we learned much more about Khushil and his diagnosis, how he was only given nine months to live, but exceeded this by two and a half years! The bravery and strength of the family and young Khushil touched us all. Khushil will remain in my thoughts, and I hope he will continue to inspire others.

Alison (Funeral Director – Co-Op Funeral Director)

I first became aware of Khushil being in our care through a telephone conversation with Charlotte. The loss of a young child is catastrophic. Our role from the outset is always to bring the loved one into our care, and care for them and their family. We never lose sight of the privilege or responsibility that this brings. We also play a hugely supporting and guiding role to the family, and will do whatever we can to lessen the burden of their loss. At this point, I don't think that the full extent of Khushil's illness was known to us. It was tragic enough that such a young boy had lost his life. It was only through our developing relationship with his parents and Namrata in particular, that the details slowly began to unfold.

Charlotte was to visit Khushil's parents at home, and begin the funeral arrangements with them. Earlier that morning, Khushil had been brought from his home by our colleagues, Peter Kilday and Paul Hamilton. From experience, these are emotionally demanding times for the families and ourselves. Finding the right words of condolence and support, building trust and confidence in the family and gauging how much the family can cope with, can be a minefield. We have to trust in our experience and instinct, to ensure that we get the balance right.

I first saw Khushil when he had been unconfined, and was to be taken over to the funeral home to rest. He was in Charlotte's care, and his mum and dad were told that they were able to visit whenever they wanted. If this is the wish of the family, time together is invaluable. My first reaction when I saw Khushil was that I wanted to cry. I am a Mum first and foremost, too. Khushil was the same age as my young son, which made it harder to deal with. However, Khushil looked very peaceful, dressed as any young teenage boy would dress.

I met with Khushil's mum and dad a few days before the funeral. They had asked for him to be bought home for a few hours, before the service at the crematorium, so they could hold a religious service. When I met with Khushil's parents, I was struck by their calmness and dignity. We chatted briefly about Khushil and how he approached everything with great determination, attention to detail and how he was a stickler for timings. I remember in a light-hearted moment with Namrata saying how we had better remember that on the day of the funeral.

I checked the route that we would take around to the back of the house with the coffin, to where it would rest in the house. The neighbor had scaffolding up, and was keen to stress that if anything needed to be moved then they would do whatever they could. Everyone wanted to do whatever they could to make sure Khushil could be bought home. From what I could see, no adjustments were needed, and Khushil would be home for his final few hours on Saturday. I then had a chat with the parents, and talked through the day of the funeral with them. I knew that they wanted us to take Khushil past his school, where his friends and teachers would be lining the route as he passed. School was very important to him and this never lessened throughout the time he was ill. The route being lined by friends and teachers was also a fitting tribute. His best friend Hem would also join me, as we walked the hearse down past the school. After I said goodbye to Khushil's parents, I drove the route a few times, just to have it clear in my head for the day of the funeral.

On the day, I remember getting up early. Inevitably, your mind turns to Khushil and his family, and I remember reminding myself that no matter how I felt, it could not compare to what they were going through. All five of the people (including myself) who carried out Khushil's funeral were parents too. The tragic circumstances of Khushil's death were felt by us all. Out of respect to Khushil, I knocked on the chapel door and we made our preparations before leaving to take Khushil home. It was impossible to lose sight of the sadness at seeing Khushil at rest in his coffin. As I checked his ID bracelet, I remember talking to Khushil as if he were one of my own children. I carefully made sure that I put back his shirt sleeve properly, and tucked in his SpongeBob SquarePants teddy, so they were both resting comfortably together. With our checks done, we placed the flowers on the coffin and the others in the hearse. I paged the hearse, passed the front of the branch, and paid my respects by bowing to Khushil at the head of the coffin. Then we began the journey that would take Khushil home.

I remember there being many people at the house, and I can recall speaking with Khushil's mum and dad – again both were incredibly calm and dignified as their son was bought into his home. We placed the coffin according to the wishes of his mum and dad. The coffin was opened, as requested. We paid our respects, and then respectfully withdrew, to allow the religious ceremony for Khushil to begin.

Once the coffin was closed for the final time, we took Khushil from his house, feet first as his parents had asked, and placed the coffin on the hearse for Khushil's final journey.

We had a short journey to make to the school, with Khushil's parents and other mourners following behind.

Khushil's friends and teachers would be waiting, and lining the route that we were to make past his school. At the top of the road, Khushil's best friend Hem was waiting with Mum. Hem was to walk in front of the hearse with me. This was a very courageous thing for Hem to do, in tribute to his best friend – he never faltered as he walked beside me. As we walked past the many children and teachers that had turned out to say farewell that day, I couldn't help thinking about what was going through their young minds.

The service was to be about an hour long, and then the family were to witness the charge of the coffin. The chapel was full, as I recall. We carried Khushil into the chapel, and placed the coffin on the catafalque. We then paid our respects to Khushil, and left the chapel, so the service could begin.

I always make a point of being outside the chapel and listening to the service. I am there in case anything goes wrong, and to wait for the family as the service finishes, and also to learn about the person whom we have looked after and cared for. As I listened, it was evident what a remarkable boy Khushil was. He had faced his illness with tremendous courage, determined to achieve all he could. His attendance at school was remarkable despite having to undergo radiotherapy – even attending school straight after treatment. He was still asking for school work when his teacher paid his last visit to him! It was impossible not to be caught up in the emotion of the service. I think it was during his mum's tribute that she mentioned how he had insisted on completing his Duke of Edinburgh award, and refused all offers of her help! My daughter had completed the same award, and I appreciated what was required to achieve this. I broke down in tears, and stood by the outer doorway trying to compose myself before I went back into the chapel.

It was an absolute privilege to be asked to contribute to this book. There was only one hero on that day – and that was Khushil. We were quite simply doing our job. Whilst Charlotte and I fronted the care in the funeral home, and on the day, we can by no means take the credit for those words spoken by Namrata. The funeral, as she described it, was 'perfect'. This meant a great deal to me, and will always be cherished. We were both supported by our colleagues, many of whom work tirelessly behind the scenes.

As we go about our work, it is very difficult not to be affected by the families we care for, and the circumstances that lead them to us. Khushil and his family are no exception to this. From talking to Khushil's mum, you cannot help but think that it was his sheer determination not to be defeated, and to strive for a fulfilling life for as long as possible, that carried him through – well beyond the doctors' predicted time frame. As a mum, I cannot begin to understand how you cope when you are told that your child has only months to live, and there is nothing you can do. I only hope that in the account I have given, I have done justice to the privilege it was to care for Khushil, and that I provided a fitting funeral for such a remarkable young boy.

Namrata has shown immense strength and determination in telling Khushil's story. I hope this book provides a voice for Khushil and other children who are suffering with this terrible disease. I hope these voices are heard, and are the vehicles for change. Together, we can secure funding for DIPG research. Together, we can make the suffering stop, and ensure that the lives of children are lived in the way they were intended.

A Final Word From Namrata

Please email me, leave your comments on Facebook, or Twitter, and don't forget to visit my website The Khushil Pandya Fund and charity page for your donations. Share the link with as many friends and family as possible.

We would really appreciate it if you could leave us an honest review on Amazon. You can find the book by searching ISBN 9781527228870.

Help us to find a cure for this deadly cancer, and stop parents everywhere from losing their cheeky, loving, superstars.

 The Khushil Pandya Fund

https://thekhushilpandyafund.org/

https://www.justgiving.com/fundraising/
thekhushilpandyafund

https://www.thebraintumourcharity.org/get-involved/
our-supporter-groups/supporter-groups/groups/
the-khushil-pandya-fund/